Thanks

I'd like to thank the all the users of Reddit who asked these questions and also thank the people who took the time to reply with informative, insightful or humorous relies.

Bio

I'll try to keep this short and sweet to avoid boring you to death. So this is my first published ebook and I plan to make a few more volumes of it when I get around to it. I hope that if you find any of this interesting that you may want to get another one.

I am an English teacher who has been living and working in South East Asia for around 6 years now and it's great. The weather, the beaches and just meeting people from all walks of life is great. So I hope that by you purchasing this book I can continue to travel and have a few cold beers along the way.

Thanks ~ Darren

Table of Contents

Anthony Bourdain (Travel/Chef)
20th September 2016

Charging55
**How do you find the local experts in 'No Reservations"
and how difficult is filming in countries that are not
friendly to Americans in general?**

We're very very good. I've been working with the same people
for the whole time I've made television. And we've been
traveling together and doing this thing for many years, and
we found out really early on that the person you select to be
your fixer in those countries, in any country, determines the
success or failure of the show. So we're really really careful
about finding these people who, generally speaking, are
professionals who work with either news outlets, people
shooting or filming major films, shooting commercials; we
audition them over Skype and email; we make sure that they
have an understanding of what show it is we're making and
what show we're *not* making. It's really important they
understand we're not looking for the "Top 10 Best Places" in a
particular city. They have to have a sense of humor, and they
have to be as knowledgeable of the places as they *claim* to
be, which is something that has been a problem in the long
ago past.

We just learned to be good judges of character in a solid fixer.
Man, that will literally save your life, and has in our cases
many times. We would not have made it intact out of Congo I
don't think without a really great fixer. And in fact, we got
everything we needed to there.

It's difficult in countries where you know that they are
possibly more paranoid. Mostly people from the security
services give us drivers or translators whose job it is to keep
an eye on us. We're pretty good, and they may want to steer

us to see positive aspects of their society, and try to get us to play into some agenda. We're pretty good at avoiding that and seeing through that. A lot of times we'll do some of what they call "French shooting" which, yes we'll let them take us on the dog-and-pony show, and we'll pretend to shoot it, but never actually end up using it on the show.

Generally speaking, people have been pretty nice to us around the world, but we do understand if you're in China or Iran, for instance, you cannot point your cameras at military installations or secret police who are walking by. It's probably not a good idea to put a camera up to those. We also have to be very careful about the position we leave our hosts in. Meaning, I can go around and come back and say anything I want about the place; but all of the people who are nice to me there, I have to think about the repercussions of my comments here. And we're very careful about that as well. I can say what I want, but I have to think about the people who were kind to me and trusted me in countries that take a dim view of free speech, let's put it that way.

oppleTANK

1. **Which ethnic food do Americans need to embrace more?**
2. **Which foods do Americans need to stop eating?**

There are a lot that I think are underappreciated. Chinese food still remains a mystery to us, it's not really anything like what they eat in China. Our knowledge on Japanese is not so wonderful. Countries who's food is underrepresented, Brazil, Peru, higher end Mexican food, Burmese, West African. Food from Senegal and Ghana is amazing, delicious, complex and interesting. So many of the fundamental flavors of what we call american food, in fact, came from those places. "Traditional Southern Food" so many of those textures and flavors and ingredients can trace their roots directly to West Africa.

Well look, do you really need pizza that's stuffed with cheese? County faire novelty food? deep fried butter. We can eat a lot less deep fried stuff, for sure. I'm not a big fan of the major fast food chains. Anything that's oversized. Giant jugs of soda.

I'm a father and I think about these things, sugar intake. I'm gonna be fair to junk food, I have trashy taste, but some of the fast food concoctions are pretty heinous. I personally don't like fake Italian or fake Mexican food. One of the joys of having lots of Mexicans and Mexican Americans around is they make delicious food! Why would we go a to a fast food outlet, for more money, selling us bad food. I wouldn't mind seeing the end of these monster nacho concoctions. Anyone who would insist on putting BBQ in a Nori roll, kind of offends me. Theme restaurants...not so great. There is a restaurant in Vegas, I think it's called The Heart Attack Grill, where if you are over 350lbs you eat for free. I think that should be pretty much a war crime.

Griffin3141
Tony, you really inspired me to travel the world. I spent 6 months backpacking in Southeast Asia last year and always made a point to seek out restaurants you'd visited. Thanks for what you do.

That said, how do you feel about the impact of a small local restaurant appearing on your shows? Do you ever make a point to not reveal the location of a restaurant?

I remember visiting the Soup Lady in Saigon, and it had become a pretty big tourist hot spot. This wasn't the case everywhere you'd been, but the impact was definitely visible at times.

Yeah, that's a hard question that we wrestle with all the time on the show. I understand there are places that I love because they're sort of untouched, beloved by locals, undiscovered. That's exactly the type of place I love to celebrate. On the other hand I understand that very often the fact that we put those places on TV changes the nature of the business. Next time we go back there are tourists there, they added an extra dining room, the place is less charming. I imagine the locals, who have been going there for years, are kind of pissed at us.

There have been occasions where someone has taken us to a special place of theirs, that is just so awesome, and they express have reservations about putting it on TV. They don't want to see the place ruined. We have referred to places as "restaurant X" or said "we're just not telling you the name of this bar." A few people do the extra work to find the place, at least they have to work extra to find it. There are places that are just so awesome that I will just look into the camera and say "look I'm just not telling you where this place is or what it's name is. I just don't want to ruin it." More often than not, there is an element of destroying the things I love.

What food trend do you want to see die quickly? And what would you like to see become a food trend?

I would like to see the pumpkin spice craze drowned in its own blood. Quickly. Juice--I don't understand the juice cleanse. I mean, if you've ever had a colonoscopy, the doctor gives you something that will cleanse you right quick, so I don't really understand juice cleanses. I believe celiac disease is a very serious ailment, and if you're diagnosed with it, I'm pleased that there are now gluten-free options, but these people who are treating gluten as, you know, an equivalent of Al Qaeda are worrying to me. So, I'm uneasy about that.

Also, overuse of the word "artisanal". You know, an artisanal potato chip? What does that mean other than it's an expensive potato chip? Oh, I'm also no big fan of the judgmental barista and beer nerds. I mean, I like a good craft, but don't make me feel bad about my beer choices. You know what kind of beer I like? I like cold beer.

I would like people really to pay more for top-quality Mexican food. I think it's the most undervalued, underappreciated world cuisine with tremendous, tremendous potential. These are in many cases really complex, wonderful sauces; particularly from Oaxaca, for instance, that date back from before Europe. I'm very excited about the possibilities for that cuisine, and I think we should pay more attention to it, learn more about it, and value it more. This is frankly a racist assumption that Mexican food or Indian food should be cheap. That's not right.

Attorneys suing the FCC over net neutrality (Legal) 25th September 2017

Scottsummerstheyouth

Hi, can you explain to me a little more about your case? Thanks!

Millions of comments have been submitted to the FCC regarding net neutrality and we still don't know how many of those comments are fake. At the beginning of June our client, Jason Prechtel, submitted a FOIA request to the FCC seeking records that would reveal how many of the comments are fake and/or submitted by bots. The fact that the FCC has repeatedly chosen not to fully explain the problems with their online public commenting system and instead let the process continue for months as if nothing was wrong is both suspicious and concerning. The people who had their personal information stolen and fraudulently used to post online comments without their knowledge have a right to know and are still waiting for answers. The FCC hasn't even given us the decency of a response to our client's request. Instead, they are violating the law and basically ignoring it. So we've sued.

CounterSanity

Ajit Pai's appointment as the head of the FCC is such a glaring and blindingly obvious conflict of interest with his background as an attorney for Verizon (who would greatly benefit from not having to adhere to Title II regulations). Why is this allowed to happen? Not just at the FCC, but all over the government we have appointments of people who are running organizations that they have spent the past decade vowing to destroy. Do we have any legal protection from malicious oversight?

While there are a lot of laws that the government is required to follow, the courts often don't allow individuals to file suit to enforce them. The legal doctrine is called "standing," and you usually need to show a "particularized harm." But that's a great question. We'll take a look at what specific laws might apply and whether there is a way to bring a suit. Otherwise, it's something that has to be handled politically (ie, at the ballot box). Not a satisfying answer, we know.

Smoov22
Hey! I think most of the world has a mental barrier between email and digital action against Congress and going to their local building. Whether it be because they would be too embarrassed, unable, or unwilling, most people would not do something lowly, let alone what you're doing. What can you (and I) say to convince the community to go out and take action themselves?

A lot of times people don't try because they don't think they have any chance of changing things. One of the biggest lessons from the Laquan McDonald FOIA case we handled (for an independent freelance journalist) is that just showing people the truth can actually lead to change. Thousands of people came out to protest and forced the City of Chicago to make changes to police accountability, so people should remember they usually aren't alone in wanting to hold their government accountable. There is still so much work to be done on that, but the public demand hasn't let up. So people should find that encouraging and should fight for their right to information. We're always happy to help with that!

Msatretwhaart
Let's say you're successful in compelling the FCC to comply with the FOIA request, and it proves that the comments were fraudulent. What happens then?

Let's also say that net neutrality was successfully (or effectively) eliminated, what happens then if the above scenario turned out to be true. What would happen then? Is there any precedent for either scenario? What a mess!

If the comment process was a fraud, Congress ought to make sure that can't keep happening and people need to understand not to trust those comments. DOJ should also be looking whether this was criminal.

CounterSanity

I feel like transparency in the government kind of a no brainer. There is obviously a need for operational security, but it seems like the government abuses that classification quite a bit. What kind of arguments do you guys hear from the government in defenses of their lack of transparency?

We find that the government (from the federal government on down to local library boards) usually throws a lot of legal spaghetti at the wall to see what sticks. If they can dream up any basis to withhold something that doesn't make them look like complete morons, they'll do it, even though the law is really pretty demanding in favor of disclosure. We also find a lot of scare tactics along the lines of "if you release this, judge, you'll make it easier for terrorists to attack us." But the courts are usually pretty good about seeing through the garbage. Personal privacy exemptions get over-asserted a lot, and we doubt that many government officials really are concerned about it (as opposed to trying to hide behind it to keep their own embarrassing actions secret.) And definitely law enforcement agencies dream up all kinds of fanciful ways that release of basic information would hurt their investigations that don't hold water once you challenge them.

Go_to_the_jim

I tend to think transparency is an essential ingredient to democratic health. Do you think it could be possible for a politician to push for a broad legal framework that would better access to information and transparency through all (or most) spheres of govt?

Does that kind of framework already exist in the United States (or anywhere else in the world)? If so, what makes it efficient, or inefficient for that matter?

We couldn't agree more with your first point. Generally speaking, the legal framework on transparency is pretty good. It's really a question of enforcement. It's not terribly "painful" for the government to get caught in a FOIA violation. One thing to look at is to impose much stiffer penalties, especially when agencies know darn well they are violating the law.

Barack Obama
29th August 2012

Gobearss
How do you balance family life and hobbies with, well, being the POTUS?

It's hard - truthfully the main thing other than work is just making sure that I'm spending enough time with michelle and the girls. The big advantage I have is that I live above the store - so I have no commute! So we make sure that when I'm in DC I never miss dinner with them at 6:30 pm - even if I have to go back down to the Oval for work later in the evening. I do work out every morning as well, and try to get a basketball or golf game in on the weekends just to get out of the bubble. Speaking of balance, though, I need to get going so I'm back in DC in time for dinner. But I want to thank everybody at reddit for participating - this is an example of how technology and the internet can empower the sorts of conversations that strengthen our democracy over the long run. By the way, if you want to know what I think about this whole reddit experience - NOT BAD!

Suzmerk
What are you going to do to end the corrupting influence of money in politics during your second term?

Money has always been a factor in politics, but we are seeing something new in the no-holds barred flow of seven and eight figure checks, most undisclosed, into super-PACs; they fundamentally threaten to overwhelm the political process over the long run and drown out the voices of ordinary citizens. We need to start with passing the Disclose Act that is already written and been sponsored in Congress - to at least force disclosure of who is giving to who. We should also pass legislation prohibiting the bundling of campaign contributions from lobbyists. Over the longer term, I think we need to seriously consider mobilizing a constitutional amendment process to overturn Citizens United (assuming the Supreme Court doesn't revisit it). Even if the amendment process falls short, it can shine a spotlight of the super-PAC phenomenon and help apply pressure for change.

FifthSurprise
What was the most difficult decision that you had to make during this term?

The decision to surge our forces in afghanistan. Any time you send our brave men and women into battle, you know that not everyone will come home safely, and that necessarily weighs heavily on you. The decision did help us blunt the taliban's momentum, and is allowing us to transition to afghan lead - so we will have recovered that surge at the end of this month, and will end the war at the end of 2014. But knowing of the heroes that have fallen is something you never forget.

Ormirian
Are you considering increasing funds to the space program?

Making sure we stay at the forefront of space exploration is a big priority for my administration. The passing of Neil Armstrong this week is a reminder of the inspiration and wonder that our space program has provided in the past; the curiosity probe on mars is a reminder of what remains to be discovered. The key is to make sure that we invest in cutting edge research that can take us to the next level - so even as we continue work with the international space station, we are focused on a potential mission to a asteroid as a prelude to a manned Mars flight.

Hmlee
I am recent law school graduate. Despite graduating from a top school, I find myself unemployed with a large student loan debt burden. While I'm sure my immediate prospects will improve in time, it's difficult to be optimistic about the future knowing that my ability to live a productive life -- to have a fulfilling career, to buy a house, to someday raise a family -- is hampered by my debt and the bleak economic outlook for young people. I know that I'm not alone in feeling this way. Many of us are demoralized. Your 2008

campaign was successful in large part due to the efforts of younger demographics. We worked for you, we campaigned for you, and we turned out in record numbers to vote for you. What can I say to encourage those in similar situations as I am to show up again in November? What hope can you offer us for your second term?

I understand how tough it is out there for recent grads. You're right - your long term prospects are great, but that doesn't help in the short term. Obviously some of the steps we have taken already help young people at the start of their careers. Because of the health care bill, you can stay on your parent's plan until you're twenty six. Because of our student loan bill, we are lowering the debt burdens that young people have to carry. But the key for your future, and all our futures, is an economy that is growing and creating solid middle class jobs - and that's why the choice in this election is so important. The other party has two ideas for growth - more taxs cuts for the wealthy (paid for by raising tax burdens on the middle class and gutting investments like education) and getting rid of regulations we've put in place to control the excesses on wall street and help consumers. These ideas have been tried, they didn't work, and will make the economy worse. I want to keep promoting advanced manufacturing that will bring jobs back to America, promote all-American energy sources (including wind and solar), keep investing in education and make college more affordable, rebuild our infrastructure, invest in science, and reduce our deficit in a balanced way with prudent spending cuts and higher taxes on folks making more than $250,000/year. I don't promise that this will solve all our immediate economic challenges, but my plans will lay the foundation for long term growth for your generation, and for generations to follow. So don't be discouraged - we didn't get into this fix overnight, and we won't get out overnight, but we are making progress and with your help will make more.

Karlfranks
Who's your favourite Basketball player?

Jordan - I'm a Bulls guy.

SharkGirl
We know how Republicans feel about protecting Internet Freedom. Is Internet Freedom an issue you'd push to add to the Democratic Party's 2012 platform?

Internet freedom is something I know you all care passionately about; I do too. We will fight hard to make sure that the internet remains the open forum for everybody - from those who are expressing an idea to those to want to start a business. And although there will be occasional disagreements on the details of various legislative proposals, I won't stray from that principle - and it will be reflected in the platform.

Bernie Sanders (Politics)
19th May 2015

Littlenicky174
Senator Sanders,

As a young political science student it seems many of my peers are feeling increasingly disenfranchised from politics as a whole, particularly due to increasing corporate influences in politics. But realistically what can be achieved when these interest are so intertwined with current political campaigns and current issues? Is there a way to separate these interests within a political system that seems to depend on the very same interests?

Also is it seems many Americans have a negative knee-jerk reaction to social democracy ideals, even if they may be beneficial to our society. Do you think there is a way we can discuss these issues that can bring in more people to the conversation?

Excellent questions. You are right. People in general and young people in particular are increasingly alienated and disillusioned with the political process. The middle class is disappearing, the rich get richer, young people cannot afford college, the crisis of climate change is ignored, and Congress continues on its merry way paying attention to the needs of billionaires and multinational corporations. The truth is that we are in a very difficult political moment. But despair of giving up is just not an option. I would not be doing what I am doing if I did not believe that this country could provide healthcare to all as a right; that we could lead the world in transforming our energy system and dealing with climate change; that we could make education affordable for all. My strong belief is that it is imperative that we maintain our vision of what American can be, and that we fight hard to make that happen. DO NOT GIVE UP.

Nitroxium
Hi Bernie, hispanic college kid here, thanks so much for doing this AMA... Two quick questions!

1. Do you approve of the way the USA is handling their relationship with Latin America currently? Considering recent trade deals, the drug wars amongst other things have been hurting the region, do you think there is any way of changing the way the US relates itself to Latin America for a more mutually beneficial relationship?
2. What is your opinion on the fact that the DNC has scheduled only six debates for the primaries? Since it's important to get the issues out there and get yourself to be known by the people, do you think six debates are enough? And if not, is your team working on making sure there are more?

1. Great question. Given the fact that Latin America is our next-door neighbor, I have been very distressed about the lack of attention that we have paid to Latin America. I applaud President Obama's effort to normalize relations with Cuba, a country which I have visited on several occasions. But I think much more can be done to bring the United States and Latin America closer and to improve relationships with a continent that faces many economic and social problems.
2. No I don't think six debates are enough and we will be interacting with the DNC to try to create a situation where we have as many debates as possible. There are huge issues facing our country. Candidates are entitled to different points of view. The American people need to hear a serious discussion on these issues, so I hope there will be far more debates than what the DNC has proposed.

Ndphillips
Two questions for you:

1. You have been one of the few vocal critics against the war in Iraq from the beginning. Do you think there can be just wars? And in what case would you be willing to commit armed forces into other countries?

2. Which thinkers have helped shaped your views the most?

Well, that is a very big hypothetical. Yes I do believe that there can be just wars. But, you are talking to somebody who opposed Vietnam, who voted against the first Gulf War, who voted against the War in Iraq and who believes the United States has been far far too aggressive militarily in the last many years. We have got to work with the international community not only in trying to create peaceful resolutions to conflict, but to address the underlying causes of war. This is not easy stuff. But that is the direction in which we have to move.

ImLivingAmongYou
What do you think will have to be done regarding massive unemployment due to automation permanently killing jobs with no fault on the people losing these jobs?

Very important question. There is no question but that automation and robotics reduce the number of workers needed to produce products. On the other hand, there is a massive amount of work that needs to be done in this country. Our infrastructure is crumbling and we can create millions of decent-paying jobs rebuilding our roads, bridges, rail system, airports, levees, dams, etc. Further, we have enormous shortages in terms of highly-qualified pre-school educators and teachers. We need more doctors, nurses, dentists and medical personnel if we are going to provide high-quality care to all of our people. But, in direct response to the question, increased productivity should not punish the average worker, which is why we have to move toward universal health care, making higher education available to all, a social safety net which is strong and a tax system which is progressive.

GavinraraFonara
Do you think that wiretapping of American citizens is necessary for security of America and Americans?

I voted against the USA Patriot Act and voted against reauthorizing the USA Patriot Act. Obviously, terrorism is a serious threat to this country and we must do everything that we can to prevent attacks here and around the world. I believe strongly that we can protect our people without undermining our constitutional rights and I worry very very much about the huge attacks on privacy that we have seen in recent years -- both from the government and from the private sector. I worry that we are moving toward an Orwellian society and this is something I will oppose as vigorously as I can.

Afrisker
What is your opinion about possible US ground military operation in the Middle East against ISIS or Bashar Asad in Syria?

I voted against the war in Iraq and I voted against the first Gulf War. I am strongly opposed to sending American combat troops into Iraq and Syria. At the end of the day, the war against ISIS will only be won when the Muslim countries in the area fully engage and defeat ISIS and other groups that are distorting what Islam is supposed to be about. The United States and other western countries should be supportive of the efforts of those governments, but cannot lead them. The nightmare, which I believe a number of Republicans want to see, is perpetual warfare in the quagmire of the Middle East.

Bill Gates (Philanthropy)
27ᵗʰ February 2017

Suaveitguy
What are the limits of money when it comes to philanthropy?

Philanthropy is small as a part of the overall economy so it can't do things like fund health care or education for everyone. Government and the private sector are the big players so philanthropy has to be more innovative and fund pilot programs to help the other sectors. A good example is funding new medicines or charter schools where non-obvious approaches might provide the best solution.

One thing that is a challenge for our Foundation is that poor countries often have weak governance - small budgets, and the people in the ministries don't have much training. This makes it harder to get things done.

If we had more money we could do more good things - even though we are the biggest foundation we are still resource limited.

Fortunefvrsthebold
Do you believe curiosity is a trait that is naturally inherited or a trait that can be cultivated and strengthened? If the latter, what methods would you recommend for people to develop and stimulate their own curiosity?

Good question. I think having parents and teachers reinforce your curiosity and explain what they are fascinated with makes a big difference. A lot of people lose their curiosity as they get older which is a shame. One thing that helps nowadays is that if you get confused about something it is easier than ever to find an article or video to make things clear.

Hooshtin
Hi Bill,

I'm going to become a father this summer. Do you have any advice you wouldn't mind sharing, from one dad to a dad-to-be?
Thanks!

I just went on a trip with my 17 year old son to see 6 colleges. He is a junior in High School and trying to figure out where he should go. Trips like that have been a great way to spend time together. He reads even more about politics than I do so I let him pick books for me to read.

Melinda is very creative about helping me find chances to spend time with the kids. Even just driving them to school is a great time to talk to them.

Sushideception
What do you think is the most pressing issue that we could feasibly solve in the next ten years?

A lot of people feel a sense of isolation. I still wonder if digital tools can help people find opportunities to get together with others - not Tinder but more like adults who want to mentor kids or hang out with each other. It is great that kids go off and pursue opportunities but when you get communities where the economy is weak and a lot of young people have left then something should be done to help.

Qaziee
What kind of technological advancement do you wish to see in your lifetime?

The big milestone is when computers can read and understand information like humans do. There is a lot of work going on in this field - Google, Microsoft, Facebook, academia,... Right now computers don't know how to represent knowledge so they can't read a text book and pass a test.

Another whole area is vaccines. We need a vaccine for HIV, Malaria and TB and I hope we have them in the next 10-15 years.

UncomfortableChuckle
If you could give 19 year old Bill Gates some advice, what would it be?

I would explain that smartness is not single dimensional and not quite as important as I thought it was back then. I would say you might explore the developing world before you get into your forties. I wasn't very good socially back then but I am not sure there is advice that would fix that - maybe I had to be awkward and just grow up....

Bill Nye (Science)
19th April 2017

Literse
What is our worst case scenario assuming nothing gets done to save the world and what does the timeline look like? How much is my life going to be affected? My kids? I know we need to do something, but what if it doesn't work out?

The quality of life for people everywhere will go down. There will be less food and less clean water available in the developed and the developing world. It's reasonable that this will lead to conflict: more violence, more war. Here in the super-developed US, people will have to abandon homes in Miami, Galveston, Norfolk, and other coastal towns. It will lead to defaulted mortgages and people looking for jobs inland. Where will those jobs come from? Sooner we get to work the better.

Alexcore88
To what extent do you envisage automation replacing common jobs anytime soon, on a large scale? If this is accomplished do you think it will be a current player (amazon/google/tesla), something completely left-field no one expected, or a community effort from thousands of small to medium sized enterprises working together?

Self-driving vehicles seem to me to be the next Big Thing. Think of all the drivers, who will be able to do something more challenging and productive with their work day. They could be erecting wind turbines, installing photovoltaic panels, and running distributed grid power lines. Woo hoo!

Areyouhungryforapple
Hey Bill, what's your take on our chances of becoming a multi-planetary civilization in the foreseeable future?

Infinitesimal. If you think you want to live on Mars, try living in the dry valleys of Antarctica for a few years. And to play fair, you have to bring your own air to breathe. Inhaling the local atmosphere on Mars would kill you in an instant. You'd never go outside, not really. You'd live in some dome, and when you go out, you have to be in a spacesuit, which is just another dome, only really tight fitting. Oh, and there is absolutely nothing to eat.

DavidSPumkins
Bill, What are your thoughts on Elon Musk and what he is doing for the scientific world through Tesla and SpaceX?

He and is companies are shaking things up in a great way. Some disclosure, he served on the Board of The Planetary Society for a while, but has had to recuse himself as SpaceX became Yuge. (I gave him a ride to the airport once.) The Tesla outperforms conventional gas-powered cars (as does my new all-electric Chevy Bolt). If the reused lower stage of the Falcon rockets proves profitable, it will change space exploration in great way. Go Elon! (He's an immigrant to the U.S., bt-dubs.)

Dukethetiger
Actually, I have a big question for you!

I'm sure you still very clearly remember your debate with creationist Ken Ham. I'm a Christian, but personally do not agree with his views on creation.

I'm more of a Christian scientist in that I chalk up the creativity of science to God. He's responsible for the Big Bang billions of years ago, he's responsible for the creativity behind evolution, and all of the stuff that makes science so awesome are like his fingerprints.

Now you, as the awesome scientist that you are, do you think that there is any room in science for that line of thinking? Has it ever crossed your mind that there may be a higher power at work? I won't take offense at your answer.

I can't, no one can, prove there is no higher power. It's the age-old philosophical point that one cannot prove a negative. Whether or not there is a higher power, there is no question that the Earth cannot possibly 6,000 years old. Teaching kids that idea is bad for our future. But worse, is teaching kids that the Earth is cooling rather than warming. All this is made possible in Kentucky by their having elected a creationist governor, who appointed a creationist cabinet, which was in turn enabled by a creationist judge. In any other state or commonwealth, the non profit businesses run by Mr. Ham would be in conflict with out First Amendment. it will take years to undo the wrong-headed teaching of the kids in the Commonwealth. But the longest journey begins with but a single step. Thanks for writing. If you are really in touch with a Higher Power, ask her or him to straighten these Kentuckians (and immigrant Australian) out.

Ivegottoast
In your opinion, why are so many eager to discredit climate change brought about by human activities? What are the most obvious signs that they are ignoring?

The fossil fuel industry has successfully introduced the idea that ±2% is somehow the same as ±100%. Just as the cigarette/cancer deniers, did, only global and affecting billions rather than millions. Sooner we embrace renewable energy sources, the sooner we can bring the military home and be energy independent. Let's go!

RonDeJeremy
My question is what science fact absolutely blows your mind?

You and I are made of the same material as the stars. We are stardust. Therefore, you and I are at least one way that the universe knows itself. Cue the spooky music.

DownAndOutInLondon
Hey Bill,

What are your thoughts on animal agriculture and the promotion of a vegan diet as to reduce our impact on climate change?

Plant-based diets are the future. I look forward to food preparations that are not "derivative bits," as we say in comedy writing. Instead of "coconut bacon," for example, I hope there is just delicious stand-alone coconut preparations. Cooking is a competitive business. I look forward to the emergence of new plant-based dishes.

Buzz Aldrin (Science)
8th July 2014

Orangejulius
How do you feel about people who claim you faked the moon landing?

Can you describe how the moon felt to you? (Was it an adrenaline rush when your feet hit the surface? Was it soft or hard? Could you feel temperature through the suit at all?)

Funniest moment during the mission to the moon and back?

I personally don't waste very much of my time on what is so obvious to a really thinking person, of all the evidence - we talked about Carl Sagan recently, who made a very prophetic observation. He said that "extraordinary observations require extraordinary evidence to make them believable." There is not extraordinary evidence of (as far as I know) all the claims that have been made that we did NOT go to the Moon. There are photographs from lunar reconnaissance orbiter satellites, going around the moon, that clearly show all of the experiments that we described when we came back from the moon, and they are evidence that we were there, telling the truth, you can even see a trail of Neil Armstrong's trek (not footprints really but the stirred up dust in walking or jogging behind him) to see the west Crater that we had flown over, that Neil was concerned about landing close to that - and he took photos of that and then he went back to the spacecraft. I was back inside the spacecraft at this time, but looking at the photos of Lunar Reconnaissance Orbiters, you can clearly see the evidence of Neil's trek. And he took photographs, and all the signs are still there. Our flag in Apollo 11 was, without the doubt, the best looking flag that was stuck on the moon. But it was close to the spacecraft, so when we lifted off, Neil observed that the rocket exhaust caused the flag to strike the ground, to fall over. And by this time, I'm sure the radiation in space has deteriorated every piece of cloth on the flags, whether they are flying on the surface or standing up. We perhaps in the future will have very accurate rovers that can approach the different landing sites, and perhaps make available to people back on earth the ability to control a video scan, get out elevations, with floodlights to illuminate during the 14 days of darkness - I believe this will be very inspiring to people back here on earth, if we have the funds to do that, it would be great to do that.

The space suit had a soft interior to the shoes, and when the boots got put over the shoes, there is much cushioning effect, and the light weight due to the reduced gravity and the thickness of the dust, made it difficult to sense the feel of the surface. it was so remarkable, the way the bootprints were left, with such strong definition of the soil underneath, like moist talcum powder I guess, it keeps its shape, so I photographed before and after, pictures of the surface, and then I thought that looked a little lonely, so I put another bootprint down, and moved my foot a little bit so you could see my foot and the bootprint.

I have since been told by a comic, by a humorist, what humor really is - but just as we were leaving the moon, I had given some thought to this, and I was able to create two achievements of humor in one sentence.

When Mission Control said, to us, as we were about to leave "Tranquility bass, you are cleared for liftoff," I responded by saying to them "Roger, Houston, we are number one on the runway."

There wasn't anybody else for us to be 2, 3, 4 to! But there wasn't any runway up there either!

It's a phrase most pilots hear many times - "Roger Tower, acknowledge we are number 3 for takeoff on the runway" Because there are people waiting before us in an airplane to start take off. Pilots always get it. We are not going to roll ahead with increasing speed, we were going to lift off straight UP the way we left the earth!.

iamaAMAfan
Our nation and our world have been waiting for another monumental achievement by humanity ever since you were a pioneer in the space race and set foot on the Moon. For lack of any serious government effort, I'm

rooting for Elon Musk to accomplish this by sending man to Mars. What advice would you give Elon to achieve the ultimate objective of permanence on Mars?

There is very little doubt, in my mind, that what the next monumental achievement of humanity will be the first landing by an Earthling, a human being, on the planet Mars. And I expect that within 2 decades of the 5th anniversary of the first landing on the moon, that within 2 decades America will lead an international presence on Planet Mars. Some people may be rooting for Elon - I think he could, with his SpaceX, contribute considerably, enormously, to an international activity not only at the moon but also on Mars. I have considered whether a landing on Mars could be done by the private sector. It conflicts with my very strong idea, concept, conviction, that the first human beings to land on Mars should not come back to Earth. They should be the beginning of a build-up of a colony / settlement, I call it a "permanence." A settlement you can visit once or twice, come back, and then decide you want to settle. Same with a colony. But you want it to be permanent from the get-go, from the very first. I know that many people don't feel that that should be done. Some people even consider it distinctly a suicide mission. Not me! Not at all. Because we will plan, we will construct from the moon of Mars, over a period of 6-7 years, the landing of different objects at the landing site that will be brought together to form a complete Mars habitat and laboratory, similar to what has been done at the Moon. Tourism trips to Mars and back are just not the appropriate way for human beings from Earth - to have an individual company, no matter how smart, send people to mars and bring them back, it is VERY very expensive. It delays the obtaining of permanence, internationally. Your question referred to a *monumental achievement by humanity* - that should not be one private company at all, it should be a collection of the best from all the countries on Earth, and the leader of the nation or the groups who makes a commitment to do that in 2 decades will be remembered throughout history, hundreds and thousands of years in the future of the history of humanity, beginning, commencing, a human occupation of the solar system.

15chainz

Mr. Aldrin, do you watch movies about people going to space, if so, which one is your favourite?

I have watched many movies from martians coming to Earth in New Jersey in the form of giant snakes - this was a radio program created by Orson Welles, War of the Worlds - and I've read many science fiction stories, descriptions, by Isaac Asimov, but my favorite of course is Arthur C. Clarke. So 2001: A Space Odyssey. And then later on, I managed to arrange a cruise ship departing from Sri Lanka where Clarke lived, and I was able to stay with him, talking about many, many things in the past. I wrote a book along with Neil Armstrong and Michael Collins, called First on the Moon, and the epilogue was written by Arthur C. Clarke. When I wrote *my* book of science fiction, Arthur C. Clarke wrote a one page forward that was OUTSTANDING, absolutely, as he praised our ingenuity and imagination. And when we visited, we talked about a treasure he had discovered in the ocean, and we both hoped in the future that he and I could scuba dive and perhaps retrieve some of that treasure. That never happened, unfortunately.

I thought that the movie Gravity, the depiction of people moving around in zero gravity, was really the best I have seen. The free-falling, the actions that took place between two people, were very, I think, exaggerated, but probably bent the laws of physics. But to a person who's been in space, we would cringe looking at something that we hoped would NEVER, EVER Happen. It's very thrilling for the person who's never been there, because it portrays the hazards, the dangers that could come about if things begin to go wrong, and I think that as I came out of that movie, I said to myself and others, "Sandra Bullock deserves an Oscar."

Chris Pratt (Actor)
9th December 2016

Hurdur1

How has your past as an overweight, comedic character played influenced your growth as an actor, especially now that you're considered one of the sexiest Hollywood stars?

no vanity in comedy understanding the element of my job in where I am a prop

i was confident and in good shape when i first came to LA but nobody would cast me in any well written roles. People assumed based on my looks i was an asshole and a one trick pony. I only auditioned to play the douchebag characters. my audition material would be like "Bradley, 24, you hate him immediately"

int. locker room. Bradley looks to our hero, squints his eyes, runs his hands through his thick gelled and frosted tipped hair and says, "Fuck you pussy."

that would be my audition. "Fuck you pussy." welcome to the OC bitch.

They never let me improv or do comedy. It wasn't until I built a shlubby exterior, which stood in stark contrast to my inner confidence that people gave me room to play. ,

QuickQuest312

How is Jennifer Lawrence?

What's your best memory of working with your mates in your movies and tv shows?

Top 5 movies and shows?

You're a very lovable actor and you've lost alot of weight! I'm trying to shave weight off too because of your change in GotG! Thank you!

Jen is awesome. She's funny and cool. She's refreshingly tough. She's an amazing actor. It feels good to be around her.

Best memory? So hard to say. I've been at this for 17 years. It's a dream job. No question. There have been so many unforgettable moments. I love what I do for a living.

top 5? Also very difficult. Friday NIght lights Breaking Bad The Wire Game of Thrones Dual Survival

Shinjanator
Hey Chris, big fan here! What do you miss most about working on Parks and Rec? What was the hardest part about working on Passengers?

I miss the cast and crew. I miss my friends. I miss the commute. I miss the fact it was a steady gig, all comedy, and took me 7 minutes to get to work.

The hardest part of working on Passengers would be the schedule. There were only two of us primarily through the whole shoot and we worked incredibly long hours. I was homesick a lot of the time. It was a grind.

Cam_mciver

Since you and Jennifer Lawrence have a pretty similar sense of humour, there must've been some pretty hilarious moments on set of Passengers. What is one of the funniest (or embarrassing) moments when filming the movie?

We were sitting in our chairs waiting for the next shot and a big set light bulb exploded nearby and she screamed. high pitched. very feminine.

then she immediately looked over at me and said, "Jesus Chris! You scream like a woman! Did everyone just hear Chris?"

and for the rest of the shoot i couldn't convince anyone it wasn't me. I just had to own it.

:)

emphasis_EMPHASIS
Hey Chris, you've inspired me to lose weight because funny guys can be sexy shirtless too.

So my question is: how has getting into shape changed your life? Also is having maintain your physique harder than losing the weight?

Funny guys can be sexy shirtless. But realness is more important. Exercising for health, overall physical and spiritual well being I highly recommend. Doing it to look good naked is cool, but hardly worth the sacrifice. Work on being funny before sexy. lots of women think funny is sexy anyway.

TheMightosaurus
Was it difficult to control the raptors on the set of JURASSIC WORLD? Did you have any prior training in order to not get hurt by them? It must have been pretty scary. Was it scary? I bet it was.

haha! Yes. It's amazing i made it out alive. The sequel shoots in a fewmonths. I already have nervous diahrea, diarreah, diarreeah, how the fuck do you spell that? anyways. Yeah. I"m probably gonna die on the sequel.

Bill__the__butcher
~15 years ago you were living in your van on a beach in Hawaii, jobless, listening to Dre's 2001 everyday.

Do you ever miss anything about those days? Simpler times, being able to go anywhere you want without fear of paparazzi, etc.

That was such an amazing time in my life. There are elements I miss. Perhaps most of all, uncertainty.

J1bbly
To what extent would you consider Andy Dwyer to be based off yourself?

Andy Dwyer is the personification of my comedic schtick. I have been making people laugh with that clown for years and years. Way before I ever did Parks and Rec. He not all of me. But I AM all of him, if that makes any sense.

Dori_lukey
What would you be probably doing had you not become an actor?

If I hadn't become an actor in the way I did. (being discovered by a director, plucked from obscurity, etc) I would have continued to pursue stand up comedy. probably would have tried to become an actor that way.

-InsuranceFreud-
Would you and Eminem ever do a song together?

He's been after me for years to do a song. wait, no? he doesn't know I exist? Oh. well.... probably not. simply because he wouldn't do it. haha! But I'd buy his cologne if he had one.

IslandsOnTheCoast
What is your favorite song to absolutely rock-out too? Favorite song to cry to?

To rock out to.... Pantera Vulger Display of Power To cry to... Pantera Vulger Display of Power

Mikey1221
Would you rather fight 100 duck-sized horses or 1 horse-sized duck?

what weapons we talking? If i have a gun I'd fight the big duck. But if i didn't get weapons, and had to use my bare hands i would fight 100 horses and set myself up in a situation where i have the upper hand based on my terrain like the movie 300.

whoa! movie 300 with duck sized horses! fuck yeah.

Conan O'Brien (Entertainer)
1st March 2017

Blindedbyfury
Do you have to adjust your comedy routine when traveling to a different country (in this case, Mexico) or is comedic timing universal?

That's a great question. What surprised me the most is how little I have to adjust. Especially in Mexico. The Mexican people are really funny and sharp, and they always got the joke instantly - and they weren't afraid to give me a hard time. I'm very comfortable being the underdog when I do remotes, and all the Mexican people I encountered were great and generous improvisors.

Jmsturm
How did you become friends with Jack White?

True story: I met Jack and Meg in a bowling alley in Detroit in 1999 while shooting a remote. They were part of a group of people that came over and hung out. Later, they became famous and told me they were part of the group that were chatting and drinking beers all night. I totally lucked out. Since then, I just hang out in bowling alleys looking for future rock stars.

Washingtonwriter
I know you've told a lot of Trump-related jokes, and I've seen comments of people saying you shouldn't make things so political.
Is it important to you to tell those jokes? Do you think humor can change the dynamic in this kind of political atmosphere?
Thanks!

If you look at my show since 1993, I've always made fun of the president. Trump is the president now, and I'm always going to do jokes about him. That said, the overall thrust of our humor has never been overtly political, and I still think of our show as more silly than anything else.

Mval93
What was it like to speak to former president Vicente Fox and did you take away anything that you weren't expecting from your trip to Mexico?

President Vicente Fox was very funny, and although he was talking about a serious issue, he came prepared almost like a comedian. He entirely caught the spirit of what we were trying to do, and he's a big part of the show.

Jerrodkingery
Hi Conan, I've brought a puppet to your studio audience a few times, but the last time Jeff Ross sternly requested I keep it down during the show. Why does Jeff Ross hate puppets?

Jeff Ross was molested by a puppet in 1958. When he testified in court he had to point to a human to show where the puppet touched him.

Gredlocks
Hey Conan, I'm allergic to penicillin, clindamycin, and sulfa-based antibiotics. What type of medicine would you recommend for my next infection?

You are very wise to ask me. I'm not a doctor. Next time you're not feeling well just bite into a glow stick and suck it down.

Gooboobly
Is there ever going to be a beard reprise? I wouldn't be mad about it...

I got a complete 50/50 response on the beard. Half the people loved it, half the people hated it. Since it was my kids who hated it, it had to go. Don't fear, I still keep it in the attic with my wedding dress.

Motosanders
Is a hotdog a sandwich?

Because the bread is connected, and forms a "hinge" if you will, it falls under the "taco" classification. Ergo, hotdogs and tacos are not sandwiches. The pita, however, takes us into strange territory and demands further study.

Scrapplepony
How is Mike Sweeney still alive? What sort of superfood do you feed him?

Don't make fun of Mike Sweeney - he served our country valiantly during the Korean war. We give Mike Sweeney the same hormones they inject into old Redwoods. Currently there's a branch growing out between his shoulder blades.

Schoolhater12
Conan, in 40 years time after you stop doing your show, would u consider doing conan travels as a netflix show?

In 40 years time we'll all be brains in jars connected to a giant server. But yes, my brain will travel the world.

KidneyFailure
What's the most memorable moment you've ever had on your show?

I met my wife while filming a remote on my show. And that's interesting moment #28.
The most interesting moment was a cooking segment with Jerry Orbach.

Newandcreativeperson
If you're really conan then, what's something only he would know?

I have a scar from an appendectomy on my lower right abdomen. I have three cats named Thor, Maow and Cleo and the only one I like is Thor. My ATM Pin is 1494.

MoMerry
What is the hardest you have laughed on the show?

When people like Norm Macdonald, Will Ferrell, Martin Short, Charlene Yi, Kevin Hart, Bill Burr, Sarah Silverman, etc come on, it always makes me laugh.

Khal-Stevo
How do you still trust Paul Rudd after all these years of Mac and Me clips?

It's like Charlie Brown, Lucy, and the football. I believe in my heart one day he'll do the right thing.

Daniel Radcliffe (Actor)
27th October 2014

Mad-Eye-Ryan

How does it feel to be the main character of a Story that almost defines a generation. I'm 22 and remember the final ending to the whole saga and people were crying. After watching it, it felt like my childhood had finally ended, a very strange feeling.

Did you ever feel pressured or worried that you wouldn't live up to the name?

No, it wasn't something we thought about at the time. I have thought about it much more lately than I probably ever did at the time... but yeah, it feels wonderful, honestly, to have people still come up to you and say you were such a huge part of my childhood. It's genuinely lovely. I am very lucky to be famous for something so many people loved. And there's... yeah, I always like to say that I think some people think that because I'm making an effort to have a career for myself after Potter, that they somehow think I want to *escape* Potter? And I don't, I"m very proud of what those films were, and what we did with them. And so I always like to say I am happy to hear from people who still love the movies.

I remember when I met, once, a guy who'd been in a punk band in the 70's, and then he wouldn't talk about this punk days at all to me when I was asking, he sort of didn't want anything to do with it? And I remember being really disappointed by that, and thinking of how uncool it was for him to disown the thing that made him, and I just would never do that.

Brightblueinky

Something I've been really impressed with lately is that it seems like all of the kids that grew up acting in Harry Potter ended up very grounded and intelligent (this came to mind in particular when I saw an excerpt of an interview where you questioned how quickly people sexualized Emma Watson as soon as she turned 18). Was there an environment that helped with that, or

would you attribute that more to your parents, or something else?

I would attribute it to my parents and also to the crew of the Potter films, who were very good at treating us like kids rather than as actors, as they should have done. But yeah, it's hard to say what it comes down to. I think also when you grow up in the media, you get a very clear sense of how crazy the media is, and you know - basically the countdown that Emma's birthday was to when she turned 18, or 17, or whatnot, it was insane. It was insane. And I think when you see that perspective that we all saw at very young ages, you do get an extra level of awareness maybe. But also, thank you for the compliment of saying we are all grounded and intelligent, that is very nice.

ThouShaltMakeItClap
Over the course of the Harry Potter films, you got to work with some amazing actors like Gary Oldman and Alan Rickman. Can you share any interesting stories about working with them?

Well, one of the moments in my life that will forever be... you know, immortal in my memory, would be - because Gary Oldman is a bass player, a very good bass player, yeah, and, um, I started learning bass on the 3rd film when he joined the cast. And so one day, I think actually maybe on my 14th birthday, that day started with Gary teaching me the bass line to "Come Together" by the Beatles, yeah! And you know, that was just an amazing, amazing moment. What else... Michael Gambon was always also hilarious to be around. Something not every knows about Michael is that he collects and restores antique dueling pistols. Yeah! And they're really his passion, much more than acting is, and, uh, I remember he one morning gave me a demonstration of how you would shoot a man in a duel with a 17th century pistol in one hand and his morning coffee in the other!

Yeah, so my life has been blessed with many surreal, cool moments like that.

GetFreeCash

I heard you love to read so my questions for you today are literature-related. Are there any good books that you're currently reading, and (if offered to you) would you be in a film or stage play of "The Master and Margarita"? That would be pretty cool since you've already been in *A Young Doctor's Notebook*!

Well, that's incredibly kind, and, you know, you're welcome, I have, I think, just as much fun making those films as you did watching them, so it's always lovely when people say it as if I've done them a favour and I was having the best time of my life making those films, so it was a win-win for everybody I think.

In terms of - I just finished reading SLAUGHTERHOUSE 5, which is a fantastic book, and I would hopefully be in any adaptation of Master and Margarita, I would do literally absolutely anything on that set if they would let me, but in terms of like other books I would recommend, I also read a book not long ago called "Foe" and it's kind of a reimagining of the Robinson Crusoe story, I'll leave it at that but it's a brilliant book

Lonksnarvish

Do you go on YouTube often, and if so, what do you look at? Who are you subscribed to on there?

Well, I watch a lot of sports videos and stuff like that. I think the NFL Bad Lip Reading might be one of my favourite YouTube things. I watch a lot of Ted Talks, in terms of things on the internet.

What else do i watch? That's the thing... I like all sorts of, it's great for research, YouTube, and watching Alan Ginsberg debate William Buckley, things like that. I lost a lot of time like that, because since then I've watched all of Buckley's interviews like that with Gore Vidal and Noam Chomsky... Because it's kind of intellectual heavyweight debate that is gone from television now, but is still cool to watch. And because I met him quite recently, in the last few days I've been watching a lot of Russell Brand's videos on there. I met him because he was promoting his new book in the UK. Normally I immediately distrust actors as soon as they are talking about politics, because i think it's quite self-serving, but he's *very* sincere, and I really got on with him when I met him.

Richardwrinkle
What is the weirdest thing someone has asked you to sign?

Um... well, recently a couple of people have asked me to sign a piece of paper so they can then get it tattooed. And, you know, that's pretty weird. Just because I have pretty horrible handwriting - that AMA sign was me printing, but you should see my cursive, it's not pretty! So yeah, I would advise people against doing that. I have signed a picture of Elijah Wood - and I think we've also both said in interviews that we would like each other to play each other in films of our lives - but I was on a red carpet in Japan, and this Japanese man gave me a picture of Elijah, and I knew i wasn't going to get past the language barrier to explain, so I wrote "I am not Elijah Wood, signed Daniel Radcliffe."

And then also people seem obsessed with getting me to sign baseballs, which I don't understand... Quidditch balls would be relevant, at least, but just baseballs, for no reason at all.

Electronics repair professional hated by Apple (Technology) 11th July 2016

HeWhoCouldBeNamed
Has fixing Apple products gotten easier or harder over the years?

Harder. Everything gets smaller, more glued together. The biggest issue is finding parts, LP133WP1-TJAA for the Macbook Air is over $200 from most vendors now.. this is a screen to what is now a five year old laptop. It's BS. There's no reason for this to cost so much, someone in Taiwan is getting rich from creating artificial shortages.

Crclayton
What do you think the best argument *against* the right to repair is? Your response?

The best legitimate argument against it is the ambiguity in the bill itself, followed secondly by the idea that intellectual property rights are being infringed.

I fully believe in everything the bill suggests. There is no way that this is going to lead to intellectual property being copied... every smartphone out there already looks the same, every laptop is slowly starting to look the same and this has nothing to do with schematics. The reality is that most machines are using the sample circuit from the manufacturer to do everything anyway.

Like, the boost circuit for backlight.. it looks the same as the sample circuit in Texas Instruments' LP8550 datasheet. Same for the TPS51125. It's almost the same thing, there's nothing special or unicorn-like in any of these schematics. It's just needing to know which is which on the board that I am asking for.

I would say ambiguous language in the bill. They use the word fair all the time. Who determines fair? Me? Jessa? Apple? Tim Cook? A federal judge? A state judge? The president?

Bigbrain009
Question A; What is the hardest thing you've ever had to repair?

Question B; What is the most ridiculous damage you've ever been asked to repair?

A) this is difficult to say. there is physically difficult, and then there is mentally difficult. I would say tracing down the RTC circuit fault here was one of my proudest moments.

For question B cat piss. I used to do that but not anymore. I have enough money. fuck fixing cat piss damaged machines. or puke, or any of that shit.

Miyakami
How did you get into electronics repair? How long have you been doing it?

Proper "repair" since 2007 or so when I started getting a paycheck from Avatar studios after a very long free internship process.

Just screwing around since I modded a playstation with a mail order soldering iron in a friend's basement with some really shit guide I got from IRC around 1997. If people think my soldering is bad now.. god if only I had pictures of the first PS1 I modded. I am surprised that steaming pile of garbage even turned on.

[deleted]
Love the videos and thank you for making them. I work as a independent Apple tech support doing what you might consider low-level stuff (hardware upgrades, OS/software fixes etc). How do you deal with:

a) clients who believe the one thing you did messed-up something clearly unassociated with the repair – is there any "final word" thing you say?

and

b) clients who won't go away and always have just one more question – but often not enough to start charging them for?

a) This is where having a salesman comes in handy. I can spend 30 seconds telling them the truth and they want to burn my store down, or I can spend 15 minutes with them and they want to give me a tip. It really comes down to how you say it, how you spend the time investigating the second "issue", and how you explain yourself.

As I say this business is 5% soldering and tech and 95% psychology.

b) This depends. If they are well paying clients, I'll help them. If they are nice people who just want some additional help who acknowledge that I am busy, I'll help.

If they are not reasonable/nice people, then I will make my answers more and more curt, and go back to multitasking as much as I can. People really often mirror the amount of attention you give them. For people who have no sense of tact and fully comprehend that they are wasting someone's time when that person is very busy dealing with other things, I just stop treating them as human. I might go to the bathroom while they are in the middle of explaining something, turn the air compressor on, etc. Once someone makes it 100% obvious they are trolling me, I troll them back. I never act disrespectful - I won't yell at them, raise my voice, but I will troll them. :)

DHSean

Have you gotten any weird internet fans coming into your store or stalking you?

Yes, it sucks. Everyone here has known for years, even before I had a YT channel, that allowing a call to get to my phone means getting fired. I love my staff but it's one of those things. I get that people want to talk for 2-5 minutes and ask questions but it's not sustainable, multiply that by 100k people and when would I fix anything?

But even before that anytime someone asks for the business owner by name it's bullshit. a telemarketer, a bogus collections person, etc. there has to be a very good distinct reason to get to my phone.

in terms of actually following me I believe most know better than to do that.

eatMagnetic
Why did you decide to repair Apple products? Was it that there is a bigger demand (and also higher revenue) than other devices? Is the situation about schematics and diagnostics tools from (for example) Samsung as difficult as for Apple?

Really enjoying your Youtube-Channel (and also "non-repair" stuff on there!)

A few things.

a) Streamlined product line for parts stock. No one is willing to wait more than a day anymore, if even a day anymore, for anything. If I tell someone it will be done in 2 days they will run out mad. So I can't fix anything where I have to order parts most of the time, because it will piss people off.

I can stock three LCDs and be good for two years. With PCs there are so many different models of this that and the other thing... there's no way to know what's inside half the time without opening it. And there are thousands of different PCs.. it's not possible to stock everything.

b) Money. Apple machines hold their value better(why is beyond me since so many are made like shit), people paid more for them, so they are willing to spend more to fix them. So I can make more money off the same skillset.

It's easier to stock parts for them, and it's easier to get people to pay for repairs. It's not because I like them, it just makes business easier.

Elon Musk (Science/Business)
6th January 2015

EchoLogic
Hi Elon! I'm asking three questions on behalf of the nearly 20,000-strong fan community /r/SpaceX. We consider these the best questions we'd like you to answer for us (trust me, there were hundreds more), so a response to each would be much appreciated!

1. Falcon Heavy. Some have speculated that at stage separation the Falcon Heavy center core is too far downrange and travelling too fast to be feasibly returned to the launch site. Could you go into some detail on whether you plan to use barge landings permanently for this core, expend it depending on the mission, or take the payload loss and boost back to the launch site?
2. Mars. Could you please clarify what the Mars Colonial Transporter *actually* is? Is it a crew module like Dragon, a launch vehicle like Falcon, or a mix of both? Does it have inflatable components? Is MCT just a codename?
3. Spacesuits. How does SpaceX plan to address the limitations and contribute to the advancement of current spacesuit technology to best serve humans enroute and on the surface of Mars? You mentioned in 2013 that there'd be an update to SpaceX's "spacesuit project" soon - how is it coming along?

1. Yes, the Falcon Heavy center core is seriously hauling a** at stage separation. We can bring it back to the launch site, but the boost back penalty is significant. If we also have to the plane change for geo missions from Cape inclination (28.5 deg) to equatorial, then a downrange platform landing is needed.
2. The Mars transport system will be a completely new architecture. Am hoping to present that towards the

end of this year. Good thing we didn't do it sooner, as we have learned a huge amount from Falcon and Dragon.

3. Our spacesuit design is finally coming together and will also be unveiled later this year. We are putting a lot of effort into design esthetics, not just utility. It needs to both look like a 21st century spacesuit and work well. Really difficult to achieve both.

Aerovistae

It seems you have an extremely proficient understanding of aerospace engineering, mechanical engineering, electrical engineering, software engineering, all various subdisciplines (avionics, power electronics, structural engineering, propulsion, energy storage, AI) ETC ETC nearly all things technical.

I know you've read a lot of books and you hire a lot of smart people and soak up what they know, but you have to acknowledge you seem to have found a way to pack more knowledge into your head than nearly anyone else alive. Do you have any advice on learning? How are you so good at it?

I do kinda feel like my head is full! My context switching penalty is high and my process isolation is not what it used to be.

Frankly, though, I think most people can learn a lot more than they think they can. They sell themselves short without trying.

One bit of advice: it is important to view knowledge as sort of a semantic tree -- make sure you understand the fundamental principles, ie the trunk and big branches, before you get into the leaves/details or there is nothing for them to hang on to.

Danielle_miller

I'm a teacher, and I always wonder what I can do to help my students achieve big things. What's something your teachers did for you while you were in school that helped to encourage your ideas and thinking? Or, if they didn't, what's something they could have done better? Thanks!

The best teacher I ever had was my elementary school principal. Our math teacher quit for some reason and he decided to sub in himself for math and accelerate the syllabus by a year.

We had to work like the house was on fire for the first half of the lesson and do extra homework, but then we got to hear stories of when he was a soldier in WWII. If you didn't do the work, you didn't get to hear the stories. Everybody did the work.

AvenueEvergreen
Previously, you've stated that you estimate a 50% probability of success with the attempted landing on the automated spaceport drone ship tomorrow. Can you discuss the factors that were considered to make that estimation?

In addition, can you talk more about the grid fins that will be flying tomorrow? How do they compare to maneuvering with cold-gas thrusters?

I pretty much made that up. I have no idea :)

The grid fins are super important for landing with precision. The aerodynamic forces are way too strong for the nitrogen thrusters. In particular, achieving pitch trim is hopeless. Our atmosphere is like molasses at Mach 4!

Ghostrider176
1) What is your favorite airplane?

2) What is your favorite video game?

3) What is your favorite food?

4) If you consume alcohol, what is your favorite alcoholic drink?

SR-71

Hard to pick a favorite. I tend to like FPS with a story, like Bioshock, Fallout or Mass Effect, but was also a big fan of Civ and Warcraft.

French and BBQ
Whiskey

Goofy at Disneyland for over 20 years (Experience)8th December 2016

Aaronp613
How do you survive on really hot days?

Practice actually. It was absolute torture the first month (and especially the first parade) but after a few months I got used to it and after a few years I would forget I had the costume on.

Mozziewine
Why did you quit ?

I was fired. To make a complicated story short, Donald Duck was, as usual, being a jerk and wouldn't leave my area because I had signed "Luv, Goofy" right over the bill of a Donald Duck hat. He threw a temper tantrum and as I was dragging him across the floor to get him back to his position a little kid ran out from behind the curtain at Pete's Silly Sideshow and we knocked her on her butt. The kid was fine and no one complained but Disney didn't really appreciate me dragging the costume on the carpeted floor so they terminated me.

Out_of_the_corner
What's the strangest thing you saw in the back of house areas?

Oh my god I could go on for days about that. One thing that stands out was a special event where they needed 16 Mickeys all set out in various rooms and seeing all of them backstage was really weird.

Jdmisten
what were your co workers like? is everyone filled with the disney spirit, or do people hate their jobs there like any other job?

It's really like any other job. I went through phases myself. At first, every time I farted Pixie Dust would blow out of my butt but after several years I got kind of bitter. It was all management stuff though. On set I was fine and loved it but backstage stress got to me for a while and I was big on holding Disney accountable. After about 10 years though I calmed down. I loved every single minute while on set (for the most part) and some of my co-workers will be friends for life. You get out of it what you put into it.

Tumorman
Any good stories of playing Goofy around the time "A Goofy Movie" came out?
Bonus question: Have you ever met Powerline?

Oh. My. God.

The first time some kid asked me to do the Perfect Cast I had no idea what he was talking about so I faked it. The kid didn't buy it but luckily I had an escort (that's what they called attendants back in the day) tell the kid that I already forgot it (which is bullshit if you watch the movie). They don't prepare you for details like that in training. You're just supposed to figure it out yourself. Never met Powerline unfortunately.

Joshanaitor
Hey what's the worst and best customer experience you ever had?

Ugh. Worst guest experience? It's a tie between having my life threatened at a Grad Night party one time and one time I had to tell a guest that their son was in jail for stealing from one of the stores and she did not take it very well. Best guest experience? I've got too many to mention. One that stands out is when I was working at Mickey's Character Spot at Epcot. There was an older gentleman that came up in the queue but didn't come see me, he just sort of stood in the back and watched me for a while. After about 20 minutes he came up to me and said "Goofy, I had a special friend that would want you to have this." In Goofy you have to look down in order to make it look like Goofy is looking at you so I couldn't see him but I heard him holding back the tears. He was shaking a bit but he gave me a hug anyway. I will never forget that hug. It was one of those hugs that last with you. He was crying in my arms. He had given a pin they give to family members or friends of POWs and MIAs. It's become one of my most prized possessions.

Carnageraiser
Ever bang someone in the costume?

No, and contrary to popular belief there aren't many furries in the character department. I know there are a few (I knew one of them) but it's not something that's out in the open for sure.

BertManigert
Is it true that someone gets fired if two of the same characters appear in the same area of the park?

It would depend on the situation. I've met my double on set by accident a few times over the years (it happens to the best of us) but it was just that, an accident. The only way someone would get fired (I'm only guessing here) is if they did it on purpose.

Unknownfy24
What is your favorite Disney movie?

Tough call. I'm really partial to the Little Mermaid because of Ursula but I think all in all it has to be Ratatouille. That movie has some of my all time favorite quotes, especially Anton Ego's (sp?) speech at the end of the film. I also loved Dumbo (as racist as it was) but that's because Timothy Q Mouse is probably my favorite character of all.

Gordon Ramsey (Chef/Entertainer)
19th April 2015

Abitbolgeorges
Hello Gordon, I've wanted to know what is your opinion on Michelin rating systeme ?

That's a very good question.

One thing we need to REALLY understand about Michelin is the stars are awarded to the restaurant.

So, you know, if there's one thing I've come to admire with the Michelin is that it's consistent. It's a guy who is judging you incognito. We have a lot of guys in this country, and Europe, who are a bit too familiar, too chummy with chefs, and they overindulge - food editors, they'll know, and tip off the chef. With a Michelin guide, you have *no* idea when they'll be in, or when they'll review you. And that's why they're the most feared and respected by chefs.

Now I'm always asked - you're a hands-on chef, you're on TV, how come you're still with these stars? Who does the cooking when you're not there?

When I'm not there, I have trusted proper chefs - like Clare Smyth, the chef de cuisine in Chelsea - even when I'm there, she's still running the ship. She's been running it there for 10 years.

So the stars are awarded to the restaurant. And sometimes the chefs think the stars belong to the chefs, but they belong to the restaurant. The service is just as important. Michelin's had a hard time in America, because it was late coming to the table. But if there's one thing I respect, it's consistency. They manage to identify consistently, and it's all there for the customer.

So when people ask me "What do you think of Michelin?" I don't cook for the guide, I cook for *customers.*

Burnthebridgex
Earlier in your career, did anyone handling the media aspect ever try to convince you to change your

persona? Do you swear just as much in everyday life (please say yes)?

I've never really worried about the sort of media profile, early on in my career? I'm a chef. So I, you know, we don't get taught how to handle the media properly! And as you can probably understand, chefs when they start out make some pretty big mistakes in terms of saying things in the heat of the moment that get taken out of context, but I've always said that's passion.

Do I swear? Two weeks ago, I was at a parent's meeting for my school. And my daughter said *"Daddy, please don't embarrass me."*

SO I get to the school and the first thing that happens - there's all these mums and dads there, and all the teachers are there, with the names on the table, and I see the headmistress, and my daughter Holly was there, and it's *incredible* - I went straight up to the headmistress and asked for a selfie! Which I thought was fucking brilliant.

My daughter dived under the table in embarrassment. But it just broke the ice. These things are just so formal.

And the headmistress said *"Oh my LORD, I've never had a selfie before! What do we do!?!?"*

So I said "Put your head up and fucking smile!"

I tweeted it out. God bless 'er.

Jichh
Hey Gordon, big fan! I'm genuinely curious: how the hell do you manage your time? You are everywhere, you have at least 200 shows, a family, restaurants etc. How do you balance all that?

I...I multi-task very well.

And I am never in one place too long.

I think now with, you know, my own production company, I'm very lucky the schedule works around my diary. I work my ass off - you know, 15, 16 hours a day. I quite enjoy the time difference when I finish, for instance, last night we were taping MASTER CHEF until 9 or 10 PM at night, I'll have a quick bite to eat, and then I'll call the UK at midnight - because come midnight LA time, West Coast time, it's 8 o'clock in the morning. I'll say good morning to the kids, I'll catch up with my business in London, and then from 2-5 o'clock, I sleep, get up, go to the gym, and then start my day again.

So that's my daily slog.

So I stand by my convictions - when I opened up the restaurant, Gordon Ramsay, back in September 1998, I decided I was going to work my ass off. My flagship restaurant in Chelsea has never been open on a Saturday and Sunday - it's never been open on a week-end, because I thought if we're going to do this, I'd like to do this properly, so my staff needs time off. So I work hard, but I give myself time off on the week-end. I cut it off, and power down for 48 hours.

Funyunsgood
Do ALL the kids on Master Chef Junior really know the techniques off the top of their head for every challenge, or do you give them a quick overview/rundown before the challenge starts. For instance the crouqembouche challenge?

That's a really good question.

So across the filming procedure, we get the chance to spend time with them, with basic culinary lessons. So they won't know *exactly* what they're doing, but we'll show them basic techniques a few weeks prior. And also, things like the croquembouche - we'll do a class in sheet pastry, but we'll do sheet pastry BUNS, as opposed to actually doing a croquembouche.

When it comes to the more serious elimination challenges, they'll have insight 3-4 weeks out. We are halfway through shooting season 5 of Master Chef Junior, and I am staggered by the level of competition. We start taping tomorrow morning, but based on the standards of the first few seasons, the level is just amazing - they are coming in better, stronger. And for kids to have ballet lessons, soccer lessons, that's something we've grown up with. And I've never known kids like we're having now, who are having cooking lessons outside of school hours.

Qreib
What's your favourite Disney movie?

My favorite Disney movie.

Ehm, come on?

Seriously?

It has to be RATATOUILLE.

I was very close, last year, when we had Bradley Cooper in the kitchen cooking up a storm for his new ADAM JONES movie coming up the end of this year, and understand his level of excitement about service, being on the line - he didn't want to tiptoe, he wanted to be in there, from first light to the last plate leaving the kitchen, and it was so nice to see how he respected the team. He didn't want pampering, he wanted to roll his sleeves up and dive in there.

He said "Gordon, I just want you to teach me to put food on a plate, because it's really magical how you put food on the plate the way you do."

So I'm very excited for this movie, coming out, called ADAM JONES. It's very exciting to see an actor understand what you do, and knowing that he can't learn how to cook in a few months, but absolutely *nailing* it when it came to the level of presentation.

Holocaust Survivor – 92 years old (Experience)
3rd April 2016

PM_ME_UR_CHESTHAIR
Hey Mr. Flescher. What did your moment of liberation feel like? The day you got to leave the camps and start a normal life again. Did you ever feel like that day would come?

I didn't know it. I didn't understand. I was on another death march at the time from Altenburg to Waldenburg. I managed to slip away and hide in a chicken coop along the way and at that time the American convoy was advancing. I saw an American tank and an American soldier and thought he was going to kill me because I didn't know the uniform. I still left the coop and went up to them, because at that time I could barely stand up and weighed about 70 pounds. I was liberated on April 11.

I didn't know that day would come. I was very sick when I was liberated and could barely eat, talk, or walk.

Frentis
How did you keep going, when it was hard? Not it it wasn't hard all the time, but as a young man reading about it, I always find myself in wonder of how people got through it.

Secondly,why did you keep the tattoo? I have meet a couple of other Holocaust survivors with the tattoos themselves and heard their reasons, so I'm very curious to hear yours.

I lived for tomorrow. I was always positive. They told us if Germany won the war you'd work until you die, and if they lost the war they'd kill everyone. We are born to die, but I always kept my mind positive. I'm lucky I made it out, but I lost many family members and friends during this time.

It's important to remember the past. If I removed the tattoo it's removing a part of history. The Germans wanted to remove tattoo's from survivors afterwards, and I'm sure many people did. But it's a testament to the past. It shows I survived. And I'm here, and loving life!

LukeTheAnarchist
How were you treated in the camps? Is everything we hear about yhe holocaust true, or is some exaggerated? At what time were you placed into the camps, and when did you get out? What was daily life like? How do you feel when people today compare things to the holocaust?

We worked 12 hours from 6 to 6 everyday. We were not treated well, as you can imagine. I helped build bridges in Peiskretscham, I also worked in a shoe factory in the beginning in Ottmuth. Nothing is exaggerated. When the war broke out, I moved to Brussels with my parents. My brother got a visa in 1939 and moved to the United States. I was too young to obtain a visa, being only 14 at the time, and stayed in Brussels until I was about 16. In 1942 I received a letter to go to labor camp, and at that time my parents tried to smuggle me out of Brussels to go to Spain. While I was being smuggled out, I was caught in Lyon while buying grapes at a market along the way. Somebody asked to see my passport and right away they saw a big "J" in my passport and I was arrested. This was in 1942. I was liberated April 11, 1945. I also had a sister who was older than me, and she had a young child. She was caught around the same time as me, and was immediately sent to Auschwitz.

When people compare things today to the Holocaust they cannot understand. People live normal lives. Most people do not understand the meaning of being hungry or being cold. I was on a death march from Blechhammer to Gross Rosen and we didn't know where we were going, didn't have anything to eat, and marched in the freezing cold for two weeks. Anyone who fell was immediately shot and killed. Being hungry and cold was an afterthought when all you're trying to do was survive.

Beautyberry1

I am a pre service history and English teacher. What is something you'd want all teachers to talk about when teaching their students about the Holocaust?

They need to tell story as it is. You cannot shy away from history and its brutality. We usually learn about history through books, but this is an event that happened in my lifetime, I witnessed it, and I am still alive today to discuss it. Soon, there will not be any survivors left. I am 92. Once all the survivors are gone, the skeptics will probably come into the picture unfortunately. And that is why we need to educate everyone about what really happened. It didn't happen 500 years ago. It happened in my lifetime.

Jumpup
What was the ride to the camp like, were you aware of what awaited you, and if not when did you realize ?

I was first sent to Drancy, a transit camp. I was then transported in a cattle car packed with people with no food or water and one bucket in the middle to use as a toilet. I was 16 18 at the time. The smell was unfathomable.

After six days in the train the train came to stop. The guards started to count men. They selected 300 men. I was number 298. We were taken off the train. The train then continued on its way to Auschwitz and everyone was killed. I will never forget the number 298.

It_is_burning
You mentioned you were 70 lbs when you were liberated. I'm a dietitian and have an interest in those initial weeks when you began to eat more. Was there any process for refeeding people that you are aware of? What did your diet consist of after you were liberated? How long until you reached a normal, functioning weight?

Some people ate too much and got very sick from that. I ate slowly and slowly recovered. It took maybe four to five months to get back to a normalish weight.

Ian McKellen (Actor)
15th July 2015

Canslli
I know it's probably a common question, but how do you feel about playing Sherlock Holmes, a character so famous and beloved by many generations? And how do you compare it with more modern takes on Sherlock Holmes, like the ones made by Benedict Cumberbatch and Jonny Lee Miller?

The simple unique idea of Mr. Holmes is that he is not a fictional character. Was a real person. We meet him first at the end of his life, when he is looking back at the mystery that sent him into retirement.

So my Holmes is different from all the rest in the the is so old. He is a real man. And the Holmes everyone thinks they know through the Dr. Watson Version is incorrect. So it's a mystery to learn what mr. Homes was really like. I loved playing the part.

Mayphoenix
I cannot wait to see "Mr. Holmes." My question for you is in regards to your role on "Vicious" where your character reminds me of Peter Wyngarde, an actor who -- in the early 70s -- suffered public ridicule when it was discovered he was homosexual. Are you acquainted with him? Also, how did Freddy fare during those years when being gay in the UK was a criminal offense?

I used to live at the end of a terrace of old houses in London. And Peter lived at the other end, and indeed still does - though we are not in touch. Gay actors of his generation were subject to shameful treatment.

A characteristic I like most about Freddy and his partner Stuart is their longevity. They are survivors who deserve all the happiness they can get in their later years. Perhaps they liked being vicious to each other because the world has been vicious to them.

TheDudeNeverBowls

I recall Elijah Wood on the daily Show I think talking about matching tattoos of the runic "9" that you fellows had gotten during filming. That story touched me as it truly demonstrated the bond you guys had created while filming.

Do you fellas all keep in touch? Do you ever have reunions of the Fellowship despite your busy schedules?

We planned to meet each year once filming was complete. But so far we never have - unless of course, the other 8 are meeting without letting me know... :)

The one I see most of, is Orlando Bloom. When we were both acting on Broadway we had adjacent apartments in New York City.

Space_cheese1
Hi Sir Ian! What was your favorite memory from on set The Lord of The Rings movies?

Many. Many. Many. The scenery that was built in the studio was sensational. And I think my favorite set, that I didn't act in, was the golden Liar, where the dragon was hiding. Hundreds of thousands of golden coins, specially made.

And if you don't tell anyone, I can tell you that I have some of those coins. Along with the front door key to Bag End, which i know Peter Jackson is looking for, but will never find.

Tarradiddles
There is a rumor that Christopher Lee always wanted to play Gandalf, but you got it instead. Is there anything that Christopher Lee did that you always wanted?

It's not a rumor, it's true. He told me at our first meeting that he always thought he would be good casting as Gandalf. It turns out he was better casting as Saruman. Of all the parts he played, the one I hankered after was Sherlock Holmes. Im sorry he doesn't get to see Mr. Holmes, the movie, I think he would have enjoyed it.

I_swear_Im_innocent
Sir Ian, what is your go to home cooked meal?

I'll give you the recipe.

Slice potatoes thinly. Slice onions thinly. Grade some strong cheddar cheese. You slice some small tomatoes. And you layer those ingredients. And put them in a medium oven for one hour. And to make sure it's delicious as it always is, pour a little single cream over the potatoes, which should be the top layer.

Very comforting, quite nutritious, easy to make. Astound your friends.

Two_off
Which role did you have the most difficulty getting into?

There's usually for me a moment of despair for every part I play, worrying that I will ever convince myself that I inhabit the character. The worst case of that was "Wild Honey", based on Anton Chekov's first play. I tried to leave the production at the dress rehearsal. It's one of the biggest successes I ever had at the National Theatre in London. So, what do I know?

AlderaanRefugee
Have you talked to Michael Fassbender (your younger Magneto self) in regards to him playing MacBeth? I imagine a famous Shakespearean actor like yourself could have offered support and maybe influenced his performance.

No I have not talked to Michael about McBeth, and don't expect to. He's giving his own performance and I think it might be confusing.

You don't want to be bothered with what someone else did. You want to do your own performance.

The1RGood

How has your relationship with Sir Patrick Stewart impacted your career, and your life?

Patrick and I have known each other since we in the Royal Shakespeare Company in the 70s. Im the guy who advised him not to do Star Trek. We've recently become friends through X-Men and we did two plays together. and I married him to his lady Sunny. So all and all we've become very close to each other.

Jane Goodall (Science)
13ᵗʰ September 2017

ArtDSellers
We keep destroying our environment and the beautiful creatures that share it with us. How do you keep your chin up and remain optimistic about where humanity is headed? It's tough these days, and I'd love to hear your perspective.

As we look at what is happening in the world today, it is very, very grim. And because of that, a lot of people feel helpless, feel hopeless, and so they do nothing. And they fall into apathy and despair. So I have reasons for hope. I will share them quickly. One is the energy, commitment, and determination of young people and they are empowered to take action in programs like Roots & Shoots. Secondly, the human brain. We have this extraordinary weapon. We are finally beginning to use it to create clean green energy and find a new way of interacting with the environment and live in harmony with the other creatures. It's very strange, in fact the most intellectual creature to ever walk the planet is destroying it's only home. And I believe there's a disconnect between a clever brain and the human heart and compassion. Only when the head and heart work in harmony can we reach our true human potential. And this, I believe, is to come. From the resilience of nature, we can help to once again support life. Animals are on the very brink of extinction and we have to give them another chance. Next there is social media, which as we all know can spew out a lot of rubbish and misinformation. But, used in the right way, it means that for the first time in human history, we can bring people together around the world who all care about a particular issue like climate change so that there can be hundreds, thousands, millions, eventually billions of people all raising their voices and demanding change so that we can make a big difference and politicians will have two listen and will have to make change. And finally, the human spirit. People who tackle what seems impossible and never give up. It's so important to realize that every single one of us has that same indomitable spirit. We just have to nurture it and let it grow to make a bigger impact for good.

Treyisajedi93
What are you most proud to see change in the world over your lifetime?

When I flew over the national park in the early '90s and looked down, I was utterly shocked. What had been stretching to the West Coast was now a tiny island surrounded by completely bare fields. People too poor to buy food from elsewhere. And struggling to survive. That is when it hit me. If we don't improve the lives of these people, there is no way we can conserve the chimpanzees. And that led to the Jane Goodall Institute program. We went not as a bunch of arrogant white people telling the villagers what to do to make their lives better, but with a hand-picked team sitting down, listening to the villagers, and asking them what they thought we could do to improve their lives. And that led to a very holistic program, which gradually grew and we could introduce new ways of helping. This paid off handsomely. The people in the villages are now our partners, helping us in conservation efforts. They've agreed to have a buffer between their villagers and the park to protect the chimpanzees. And the national Park, which was completely isolated, is now gradually being linked to other groups. And this program is now in 52 villages in the Gombe area, and it's in five other countries. And it is making a huge difference. Positive in introducing the youth program reaching the villages. It's probably the most important way in which we are able to conserve chimpanzee habitats. And I'll add to that, I would say we have placed great emphasis on education, helping them stay in school beyond puberty. We do this because it's been shown all around the globe that we all improve as women's education improves. One of our problems today is a growing number of humans. As our numbers grow, there are impacts and finite resources leading to more and more poverty and hunger.

Sir_Fistingson
What was the pivotal point in your career where you decided that you absolutely wanted to study primates in the field? What were the reactions of your peers?

Well, I first decided I wanted to go to Africa and live with animals and write books about them when I was ten years old. And everybody laughed at me, how could I do that, Africa is so far away. In World War II we had very little money. I was simply a girl. They told me girl students cannot do that. But I had a wonderful mother who had supported my love of animals ever since I was born, and she said to me if you really want to do this, then you're going to have to work very hard and take advantage of opportunity. That's the message I take to young people all around the world today, especially to those in underserved communities. I came to study chimpanzees because of the paleontologist Louis Leakey who wanted somebody to go with him and study them -- he believed we shared a common ancestor 6 million years ago and that we could learn from their behavior what early humans might have been like. When I discovered that chimpanzees make and use tools, and that they have complex emotions and a sort of "culture" no one wanted to believe me. When I went to get my Phd, there was a lot of push back. But I knew this was true - so I kept going.

Lvl100Munchlax
What do you want the world to see your work for?

First of all, I would like to be remembered for helping to enable people to understand that animals are like us, their intellect and they have emotions like fear as well. Because up until the mid-'60s, it was actually thought that there was a difference in humans and the rest of the animal kingdom. And it was the work coming in, the early work, showing in how many ways the very biological system DNA and so forth that really changed. The other thing I hope to be remembered for is creating an environmental humanitarian program for people with Roots & Shoots, which is now in 100 countries. It involves members from preschool, kindergarten, universities, and everything in between. Its main message is every single one of us can make a difference. And make a difference every single day. Each group chooses themselves to help animals and wanting to help the environment. To educate young people to be better students, all the conservation work and other organizations to could benefit. And we've gone so far as destroying the planet, so the main hope is that the other people will grow up and do better than we've done.

Avyroll
I am an aspiring environmental scientist. Would you say conservation of natural resources or the protection of species is more important? I'm trying to figure out where I can do the most good.

I have already said that we can make a big difference by thinking about the consequence of the choices we make each day. Like what we buy. When it comes to what we eat, there is growing evidence that as more and more people and countries around the world eat more and more meat, this is not only involving tremendous cruelty to all the animals, but it's also having the most appalling effect on the environment. People don't always realize this. For one thing, areas of the world have been cleared to grow grain to feed the animals. And massive fossil fuel is used to take the grains to the animals and to slaughter the animals. Huge amounts of water, which is becoming increasingly scarce around the world. Huge amounts are wasted changing vegetables to animal protein. And finally, these animals, like us as well, food goes in one end and comes out the other. They belch as well as pass gas. Nothing is second most, it is very, very lethal. Of course, this is all leading to climate change and other great -- it is the greatest environmental issue facing our planet. One thing that is very, very helpful is to eat less meat or become a vegetarian or a vegan

John Cleese (Actor/Entertainer)
15th September 2017

Itspeterj
Mr. Cleese,

What do you think is the most IMPORTANT joke you've ever written?

This is the most important joke I've ever heard. Nils Bohr, the founder of Quantum Physics, had a friend to dinner. As the friend left, he noticed a horseshoe nailed above Bohr's front door. He said to Bohr, accusingly "Nils, you're a great scientist. You can't believe in superstitions." Bohr answered "I don't, but apparently it works anyway."

Manfrenjensenjen
Mr. Cleese, First, I think you're the greatest comedy writer of our time. Just had to get that out of the way. Question: I read somewhere that you were working on a screenplay about tax dodgers. Will we be seeing that anytime soon?

So, you think I'm the greatest comedy writer of our time? What the fuck do you mean by "of our time"? I am working on a light comedy about cannibalism called "Yummy."

Rbendici
Is there a project you passed on that you wish you had taken, or vice versa? Thanks for all the years of entertainment!

There are three roles I was asked to do that I really regret not taking. The Robin Williams role in Birdcage, the butler called Stevens in The Remains of the Day and the clergyman in charge of the marriage service at the end of The Princess Bride.

MacduffFifesNo1Thane
As an avid fan of yours and cheese, I must ask: what is your favorite type of cheese?

My favourite cheese is melted Gruyere. Second comes Bolivian Hyena Milk cheese, but it's very hard to get except in La Paz.

Redditreviewer
If you could change 20,000 things about this world, what would they be?

The very first thing I would do would be to make pedal bins illegal. Second, I would execute anyone called Darryl. That would be enough for the first morning.

Operation_hennessey
If there were a bio-pic made about your life, who would you cast as John Cleese?

I would cast myself, provided I was not too expensive. Otherwise, I would cast Steven Seagal.

Operation_hennessey
What are your top five favourite films of all time?

This morning they are Princess Bride, The Sting, Doctor Strangelove, The Conversation, and The Great Dictator

TheCelticOne
Hi Mr. Cleese, A lot of us redditors suffer from some form of depression & Anxiety. Have you ever experienced this? And if so, what did you do to see the brighter side of life?

Never. And I wish you wusses would stop whining about your unhappiness. I'm really fed up with it. Pour yourself a scotch and pull yourself together. Go out and shoot something!

Ski-ro-dah
Will there ever be a Python movie again?

Only when the others are dead. Then I will make the definitive one.

What would you like your headstone to read?

Go away.

I've always wondered about the writing within Monty Python. I know you did your usual Python writing with Graham Chapman, but you also wrote some material with (at least) Michael Palin and Eric Idle. I don't know if you wrote things with Terry Jones. You've talked alot about what it was like to write with Graham, but what was it like for you to write with the others and was your role in those combinations a very different one from the one you had with Graham?

Very interesting question. At the start I tried to get the other Pythons to mix up the writing partnerships a bit. I thought it worked quite well. Eric and I wrote Sir George Head climbing the twin peaks of Mount Kilimanjaro, and Michael and I wrote Mr. Hilter standing in the Minehead bye-election. Nevertheless we drifted back into our original pairings, and I don't know why. Maybe Chapman was the only one who liked writing with me. I think it was a shame, I think we would've been even more inventive if we mixed the writing teams up a bit.

Julian Assange (Wikileaks)
10th January 2017

Beefshake
Can you explain your whole October?

Most of it was extremely busy, so just try and conceptualize.

I have been in an embassy siege for the last four and a half years. It's a small embassy. The embassy is surrounded by a police and intelligence operation, of which there are numerous pictures and admissions by the British state. They admit to spending 4 million pounds a year, just on the covert and overt police surveillance, not including MI5, etc. They have sophisticated robot cameras installed in different buildings, plainclothes police operating on the street and they've done deals, of which we have the paperwork, with some of the opposing buildings owned by Harrods, which is a big department store here. Harrods is owned by the sovereign fund of Qatar.

So, it's not an easy environment to work in. Spying on the outside, some spying on the inside, informers, robot cameras, etc.

Then during October, there was pressure applied by John Kerry and the US administration and other forms of pressure domestically within Ecuador, that resulted in my Internet connection being cut off and an increase in the security environment here, in terms of people getting in and out of the building easily, etc. It was wrong for John Kerry to politicize the office of the Secretary of State and try to use that for domestic political advantage by pressuring me through my political asylum. WikiLeaks does not publish from the embassy. It doesn't work from the embassy. I am political refugee stuck in this embassy because the UK refuses to obey international law and respect my asylum rights and let me leave the country. We publish from France, Germany, the Netherlands, and so on, a wide range of countries. But not Ecuador.

Ecuador is purely pressured because they are responsible for my physical security as a political refugee. Which is disgraceful. To be fair to Ecuador, they have denied that they were pressured, but that's not what our sources say. It's a small country, 16 million people, an innovative, tough Latin American country which has stood up to enormous pressure from the US and UK, but it has it's own election on February 17th and you can see it wouldn't want an allegation that it had interfered, which it hasn't, with the US election, being used as an excuse by Hillary Clinton, who was the predicted president, to interfere with the election in Ecuador.

An intense security and diplomatic situation.

During this recent pressure conspicuously and heavily armed British police arrived, which I took a photo of and which we published, parking their vans right next to the embassy, which they haven't done, since back in 2012 when the first kind of stand-off was in the embassy. It is a of show of force, presumably to make some kind of pressure for WikiLeaks to stop publishing, but we are setup to continue on regardless of what happens to me.

No one person in WikiLeaks can become a single point of failure. Why? Because we don't want to fail, number one. Number two because if that person is perceived to be a single point of failure, it places that person in danger.

Gddboygb
In 2010 you thanked people for donating money to help decrypt the "Collateral Murder" video after having solicited donations for "supercomputer time."

PFC Manning claims that the video was "was never really encrypted." Her court martial proceedings confirm that.

I know you can't confirm or deny anything regarding Manning, but do you stand by your claim that the video you received was encrypted and that you depended on donations to decrypt it? Secondly, how importantly do you value honesty when it comes to fundraising?

I can't confirm or deny anything relating to our sources there. However, yes, there is a disappeared video and that video is on the Garani massacre. Over 80 children killed in a US airstrike in Afghanistan and more than 100 people. Quite a serious video and if you search for 'Assange Affidavit', you read an affidavit about how Sweden conducted an intelligence operation on September 27, 2010 to seize three laptops, not the high security laptops, but backup laptops, that were encrypted that ended up being the only copy we had of that video. We had other copies and they were also attacked. So, that's a great sadness from us that this terrible proof of a war crime has been possibly lost to history, as a result of very difficult attacks on us. It's something that we're a lot less susceptible to now because we have a big infrastructure.

Gddboygb
People frequently group you together with Edward Snowden because you've both released classified American documents. But your motivations and philosophies couldn't be more different.

Snowden claims to fight for privacy. He's called privacy the bedrock of freedom, that one cannot be free without privacy.

You have called privacy obsolete and unsustainable. You've said that privacy has no inherent value. You appear to believe privacy and freedom are incompatible, that you cannot be free if others can keep secrets from you. You've published the credit card numbers, social security numbers, medical information, and sexual preferences of individuals of zero public interest. Two of your most recent publications are the personal Gmail inboxes of civilians, exactly the sort of thing Snowden has tried to protect.

Can you convince me that you're right and Snowden's wrong?

Edward Snowden is a whistleblower. He committed an important and brave act, which we supported. I worked with our legal team to get him out of Hong Kong and to a place of asylum. No other media organization did that. Not the Guardian, which had been publishing his material. Nor did Amnesty, human Rights Watch, not even any institution from a government. It was WikiLeaks that acted. A small, investigative publisher, which understands computer security, cryptography, the National Security Agency, which I have been publishing about for more than ten years, and asylum law, because of my situation.

We couldn't have a situation where Edward Snowden ends up in a position like Chelsea Manning and is used as a general deterrent to other whistleblowers stepping forward. Edward would have been imprisoned at any moment in Hong Kong and would have then been turned into the propaganda that if you're trying to do something important as a whistleblower, your voice will stopped and you'll be placed in prison in very adverse conditions.

We wanted the opposite. We wanted a general incentive for others to step forward. That's for philosophical reasons, because we understand the threat of mass surveillance, but it's also understandable for institutional reasons. WikiLeaks specializes in publishing what whistleblowers reveal and if there's a chill on sources stepping forward, that's not good for us as an institution. On the other hand, if people see yes, it's good for sources to step forward, then there will be more of them.

On full publication versus the sadly limited publication of Snowden files--Edward Snowden hasn't really had a choice. He has had various views that have shifted over time, but he is in a position where we made sure he had given the documents on him to journalists before he left Hong Kong. Both Edward Snowden and I assessed that it would be a dangerous bait for him to be carrying laptops with NSA material on it, as he transited through Russia to Latin America. That might be something that would cause the Russians to hold him. So he and we made sure he had nothing. Since the point of those initial disclosures, Edward Snowden hasn't been able to control how his publications have been used.

Edward has been a very important voice in talking about the importance of different aspects of them, but he has had no control. The result is that more than 97% of the Snowden documents have been censored. Enormously important material censored and while there have been some good journalists working on them, and I think Glenn Greenwald is one of the best journalists publishing in the United States, you have to have hundreds of people and engineers working on material like this to understand what is going on.

We have a different position to those media organizations that have effectively privatized and limited that material. You can't say that the initial publications had all the important docs. There have been more publications slowly as time goes by. Even some within the past two months. Those publications, for example, include ways to find interception sites in the United States used by the NSA. There are covert procedures to visiting those sites. Now, if those had been released in 2013, investigative journalists and individuals could have gone to those sites before there was a physical cover-up. That's true in the United States and it's true in Europe and elsewhere. I am sad about how the impact of the Snowden archive has been minimized, as a result of privatizing and censoring nearly all of it.

Keanu Reeves (Actor)
13th October 2014

WhatDoesYourHeadSay
My questions are mostly about your costars. Can you tell us some of your favorite stories about working with Patrick Swayze? In Dracula, you shared some screen time with 2 of my personal favorite actors, Gary Oldman and Sir Anthony Hopkins. Did you have any trepidation or anxiety about your scenes with them? Can you share some of the stories of working with them?

You know, the memory that i have of Patrick, um, at this moment, is - I remember meeting him when we were starting on POINT BREAK, and he kind of walked up and he had a big smile on his face, and he kind reached out and shook my hand, and he was just like, "Hey man, nice to meetcha! This movie's crazy great! and LET'S DO IT!"

And so... he really was, in a way, the captain of the film in the sense of how he just inspired and motivated everyone during the film. His passion and his enthusiasm, I mean, he started jumping out of airplanes while we were filming, and then he got some of the other guys who were in the gang jumping out of airplanes. I mean, he was just... this bright light.

Working with Anthony Hopkins and Gary Oldman was a great honor, very exciting, and yes, pretty scary the first time we did scenes together.

They were both very gracious, and I remember when I was doing - we went up to the director's house, for a week of rehearsals, and I just- to me Gary Oldman at the time (and continues to be) one of the greatest actors, and so for me I was just kind of watching him and trying to learn. And Anthony Hopkins was, he was very - his HUMOR, I was surprised by his humor and his quiet wisdom. He just had this wisdom and humor. It was great to be around.

AssCrust

I read somewhere that you've signed on to portray the character John Rain in an upcoming TV-adaptation of

the book series. What's your opinion on TV as opposed to movies? It seems to be getting increasingly popular for well known actors to join TV productions and I'm wondering what you like about it or why you want to try it?

And a bonus question because I don't get to ask you questions that often, what is it about John Rain as a character that makes you want to portray him?

Yeah, there's a lot of great writing, and characters, and stories being told in television nowadays. And much more than there used to be. The opportunities to tell stories, because of the opportunities to show content. And so it's drawing actors from cinema, movie actors, actors to where there's a lot of opportunities to where you can tell stories. Specifically for John Rain, I first went to it thinking that it would be - it's a wonderful series, it's 8 books, I was thinking that maybe this would be a character in one of the books to make a film, but after getting familiar, it felt like it didn't want to be a movie, it wanted to be serialized, learning more about who he was through serialization. It's perfect for that. And that's in the works.

Kleszcz
This year marks the 20th anniversary of the landmark action movie SPEED, with you, the late Dennis Hopper, and rise star Sandra Bullock. Would you care to share some of your experiences in the making of one of the greatest action films of the last 25 years?

Happy Anniversary, SPEED!

Hmm. Well, a fun day once was the day when they let us drive down the street smashing through cars on the bus. And everyone started to scream, hehe, and then laugh when it was over, and it really bonded everyone together. It was early on in the filming, yeah, but it was really fun to be smashing through cars! And with Dennis... gosh, I got to know him over the years and I'd first worked with Dennis on a film called River's Edge, and it was cool to see him again while we were making SPEED. And something that I thought I would never do in my life was have a fight scene with Dennis Hopper on top of a subway car! Heheh! And it was just - it was a *really good day.* He had such a wonderful intelligence and sense of humor. So the chance to spend time with him was one of the highlights of my life.

Uraffululz

1. **Can I still hold out hope for the live-action version of "Cowboy Bebop" to grace/bless my vision? Afterward I would gladly go blind as payment for the opportunity. Also, I'm sure you'll get some kind of royalties.**
2. **Are you, as some have speculated, truly immortal? What is the best way you've found to deal with suffering and loneliness?**

1) Um... Cowboy Bebop, yeah! For me it seems like that ship has sailed. :(Unhappy face. Sad face! I love that series, and you know, a few years ago, when it came my way, I was really hoping we could make it. I don't know what's going on with the project now. I feel like I'd have to play Spike's older brother now...

2) Gosh, when it comes to suffering, sadness and loneliness... *hmmm.* I guess I do the best I can? I'm sorry, that's a general answer. You know, it really depends on the circumstance. Oh yeah, and I'm not immortal (unfortunately).

Shivan21
How did you come to the role of Neo?

I was very lucky.

Heh.

Um, I got a call from my agent, saying that these directors, the Wachowskis, wanted to meet, and they sent me the script, and the script was absolutely amazing, and I went in to meet with them, and they showed me some artwork, of their vision, and an early version of "bullet time," and it was very exciting and inspiring, and we looked at each other, we ended up hanging out in a parking lot outside the offices just talking and riffing, and we basically just kinda shook hands - they told me they wanted me to train for 4 months prior to filming, and I got a big grin on my face and said: "Yes."

That's how it happened.

theArnoldFans1
Hi Keanu, What's a great George Carlin memory? Are you looking forward to coming back to the next BILL & TED and shouldn't GEORGE CARLIN be honored in some way...perhaps a RUFUS statue?

Yeah, it was such an honor to get to work with George. He was really nice to Alex and I. I think when he came on the set the first day, he kind of had this twinkle in his eye that was like *"What the heck is going on here?!"*

But he was, you know, he was kind of in character, he was very serious. And over the days of filming together, he just kind of started to hang out with us, we told him how much we loved his work, his comedy, and...yeah. We miss him. I miss him.

Matt Damon (Actor)
19th July 2016

Dayofthedead204

1. **How did your cameo as the punk rock singer in the film "Euro Trip" come about?**
2. **Out of all the films where you had to rescued (Saving Private Ryan, Interstellar, and The Martian), which one is your personal favorite?**

So *EuroTrip* was written by three guys I went to college with, Alec Shaffer, Jeff Berg, and Dave Mandell. And the three of them are three of the best comedy writers in the world. In fact, Alec and Jeff when we moved out to LA, we had this running joke where we had one bottle of champagne that I think they sent to us when we sold *Good Will Hunting*, or no, we sent it to them first because they had been hired on *Seinfeld*, so we would pass this bottle back and forth, we never opened it, but it was just to congratulate each other at these milestone moments in our careers. So we kind of came up together. I was in Prague shooting *The Brothers Grimm*, we were in rehearsals, and I had a wig in that movie, and so Alec and Dave and Jeff were making *EuroTrip* and they said "Will you come play this, you know, Howard Rollins kind of insane, bad version of a suburban, you know, punk band guy?" And I said "Yea, I'm in Prague". So I showed up and I'm sitting there, and I'm like "I'm wearing a wig, just shave my head, let's just go for it." and we did it, and put a bunch of piercings all over. And "Scotty Doesn't Know", the song, was actually written by one of my college roommates brothers, and in the band, one of my college roommates is actually in that back up band, Jason, is playing guitar in that group. So it was kind of a family affair.

It's tough to choose, like between films you've been in. I don't think I'm the best objective judge of any of those films. I mean *Private Ryan* was obviously the most significant in my life because it was right when my career was starting and it came out right after *Good Will Hunting*, and it did a lot to kind of position me, you know, as an actor that a studio would take a chance on. So that was probably the most influential on my life. I haven't seen the movie in a long time, I remember loving it and being deeply grateful that I was in it, and thinking that Steven was really at the top of his game, as was Tom. So that movie was always, you know I think of *Interstellar* and *The Martian* as things I made in my 40s. My life is very different, so I almost couldn't categorize those three movies. I wouldn't put them into the same basket.

Lmi6
Hi, Matt! What was the process like of co-founding Water.org? Also, has George Clooney pulled any more pranks on you since your last AMA?

Thank you for the question. The experience of founding water.org. What really happened was once I Identified water and sanitation as the area that I wanted to focus on, and that was a whole process that Bono's group DATA was really helpful with. They organized a trip for me to study extreme poverty and I went to Africa for a couple of weeks and looked at all these different things. Water and sanitation was what really spoke to me, I felt like it understood everything and I really wanted to focus there. I think what a lot of people do, I just said I'll raise money for well projects, what we would call direct impact projects. I felt like with my name I could use whatever influence I had to direct money to good places. Then as I learned more and more about it and the deeply complex nature of the issues. I felt like I could maximize my impact more if I partnered with the preeminent expert in the space, somebody who I would be lucky to partner with, quite frankly. That's what led me to Gary White. I asked him and he said yes, the rest is history. That was in 2009. To date, actually we just got the numbers in recently, we have delivered water and sanitization solutions to 4.6 million people. That number is growing exponentially because of our system of water credit. It's using the concepts of micro-finance that Mohamed Eunice pioneered and applying them to the water sector. What's great about it is our loans are paying back at over 99% and that money just gets recycled. It's this virtuous circle. Rather than spending $25 to do a well project and give someone clean water for life, in our most mature loan programs we are down to about $5 per person. That system has driven down the philanthropic cost of capital per person substantially. Thank you for your question.

D_abernathy89

- **How long does it take you to decide "yes" or "no" on a role when you read a script?**
- **What are the ingredients of your ideal taco?**

That's a good question and I don't think there's a uniform answer. Now at this point of my career it's usually less about the script and more about who the director is, but in the case of a movie like *The Martian* I read the script and I thought it was incredible, but I also thought it was really risky because for my portion of the movie it was just going to be me up there, and when Drew Goddard who wrote the script backed out of directing it because he got another job there was no director attached, and so I just walked away from the script. I just said it's too risky, I wouldn't let just anybody did this. And then when Ridley Scott said that he liked it, the decision took me all half a second. So the script is obviously important, but it's more so about the director.

The ingredients of my ideal taco, oh my god. Fantastic question. My ideal taco is actually the taco I'm not supposed to have which is the taco we have on taco night at my house. It's the crunchy corn shell with the good meat, just ground beef in there. It's all about the layering. The meats gotta be hot, and the cheese goes on first so that it melts. And then you're gonna get in there with a little bit of tomato and lettuce but not too much cause it's not a salad, it's a taco, and then you're gonna throw some avocado on top and some sour cream and then a bunch of cholula. I don't know if you know what cholula hot sauce is but it's the best. Throw a bunch of cholula on there, maybe squeeze some lime on top, and go to town.

AtotheJ2215

My question is, would you ever consider teaming up with Ben Affleck again to write an original screenplay? Good Will Hunting is one of my favorite movies of all time, and that's due to the near-perfect writing.

Thank you. *Good Will Hunting* obviously is the most influential movie in my life, and in Ben's life, and bringing it to the screen kind of dominated our 20s. It took 5 years to get it from the time we started to the time it came out, it took 5 years. So I would love to write another script with Ben; I love Ben, I love his work, he's been my buddy for 35 years. The big issue is time for us. We have a company together so we work on a lot of projects together, but to try to carve out the time is really tough. I mean we both have a whole mess of kids now, and these other days jobs. He's directing all the time and I'm off working with these other directors. The thing about *Good Will Hunting* is that we were unemployed and we weren't writing the script on a deadline either. Nobody was expecting it, so we were just these two idiots in our basement writing this thing, and now we have all of these pressures of the lives grownups have. So I would never say never because I would absolutely love to write with Ben again, and I'd love to collaborate with him on anything, he's brilliant. I'd love to be in one of his movies that he directs. The problem there is that he just keeps giving himself the best roles, so until he stops doing that and maybe just directs, none of us can really work with him.

Jess1491
What is the best advice you've been given?

I think the best advice I was given--well, I'd say two things. When I was younger, everybody told me not to be an actor, and to this day I say that to people who come up to me and say "I'm thinking of going into acting, what do you think?" I say "Absolutely not, it's a terrible idea, don't do it." because that's what everybody said to me, and I think that if you're gonna make it in this business that is so full of rejection and hardship, you need to believe in yourself despite what everybody you love and trust tells you. And it's a very personal journey, so that was very helpful. I think, you know, the advice to stay away from this career was really helpful in my own understanding that it was that important that I pursue it. The other advice that I would say, my high school acting teacher Gerry Speca had a huge influence on me and Ben and Casey. Five words he said "Just do your work, kid." and he repeated that so many times to me "Just do your work, kid." and that is kind of what I can always retreat to. That's my touchstone if, when in doubt, just focus on my work. If everything on the movie is going wrong, alright, I'll make sure that my work is tight and go from there. And that's a great place to base from, and that's a good foundation.

Casos92
What was it like working with Robin on Good Will Hunting?

Working with Robin almost defies description. He was one of the most generous, loving, wonderful people I've ever met. He had this capacity that I've never seen on a movie set. When everyone started to get tired and started to flag a little bit, he would launch into standup. We knew it was original because he was making fun of crew members and pulling them into these bits. It was like 15 minutes of the best stand-up ever that was just privately for us. Everyone would laugh and laugh and laugh and then everybody would get this boost of energy and go back to work. I'll never be able to thank him enough for what he gave us. In my heart, that's where he is, as this person that I'm deeply deeply grateful came into my life and changed it for the better.

Mike Rowe (Entertainer)
12th November 2014

SSJStarwind16
What dirty jobs did you always want to do but the network or producers wouldn't let you do? (too dangerous, inappropriate, so on)

Thanks for the encouragement. The Skilled Trades could do with a few more fans, and I'm proud to be one of them.

Regarding barriers to dirt, there have been many, and for a multitude of reasons. The segments I was most interested in doing but found the most resistance around was that of a rendering facility.

Aside from the fact that "rendering facilities" are by their very definition optically horrific, there was another concern that I had *not* considered.

That concern can be spelled out with the following letters.

M-O-B.

That's right - the Mob is still involved in a surprising number of rendering facilities. Why the Mob has such a rich history in garbage-related industries and rendering-related industries is a conversation beyond my pay grade.

I only know how relieved I was to finally find a rendering outfit that was not owned or operated by the *Cosa Nostra.*

That facility was in Northern California. And they were called North State Rendering.

To this day, I'm impressed with how brave they were in their decision to let us provide our viewers with an unvarnished look at what it takes to turn a dead cow into several hundred pounds of chicken feed.

Yes, I'm deeply proud of that day.

Nomadbishop
What job shocked you the most by finding out how awful it really was?

Many jobs appear bad at a glance, only to get much worse at a second glance.

And some jobs simply get worse and worse with every subsequent glance, which is why (of course) many people watch the program with their eyes closed.

I was never in a position to close *my* eyes, and consequently, I enjoyed a front-row seat to a great variety of pits, and holes, that most people simply don't know exist.

One brief example might be the interior of an ocean buoy.

In the Coast Guard, buoy tenders are responsible for hoisting these giant steel contraptions out of the ocean, and refurbishing them.

In this case, "refurbishment" means *"crawling into a woefully inadequate tube not much larger than the space taken up by your shoulders, and wiggling your way like a worm into the shadowy depths whereupon you begin to remove the barnacles and various other forms of nautical life with a stick or some other improvised tool."*

I could go on, but I won't.

Blyxxa

Hey Mike, what profession have you gained the most respect for over the years?

At the risk of sounding overly earnest (and too metaphorical), I'm going to say: the welder.

Welders not only work their asses off, they're in high demand, and critical to polite society. The entire world, including our infrastructure, and the building in which I currently find myself, is held together with welds.

Remove the welder retroactively from the species, and the *whole thing* shits the bed.

FunkyBunchMark

Why do you still choose to live moderately even though you have made enough money to not do so? I saw the emails online that people send you and you reply and you sent a guy a picture of your view outside your

apartment and there is a smokestack outside of it. why are you so humble??!

I'm not really humble, I'm just not properly acquisitive.

I take more pleasure in saving than spending.

And like the Native Americans, I tend to look at "ownership" as something more akin to stewardship. In other words, the more things you own, the more *things* own *you.*

On a practical level, I find if you don't have the space for a lot of stuff, you don't wind up with a lot of stuff.

Arbitrary_aardvark

Hey Mike! If you had to choose one job to do permanently, out of all the ones you tried out on Dirty Jobs, what would it be?

Hmmm.

Personally, I've never had the ability to do the same job for more than a few days at a time.

Clean, dirty, exciting, or tedious.

I simply don't have the wherewithal to stick with one vocation too long.

It is, without question, a character flaw.

Regarding the Creator's larynx, I agree that he (or she) must certainly possess a rich, well-modulated baritone.

However, for reasons that involve the Screen Actor's Guild, I must be perfectly clear about the fact that it isn't mine.

[deleted]

I really appreciate the work you do for trade activism, and the revival of blue collar trades. As someone who lives in Alberta, Canada where the trades seem to flourish, what are the biggest obstacles in the fight against the decline of the blue collar trades in the States?

The short answer is: perception.

The number of people who depend upon a workable infrastructure and a skilled trade force are coincidentally the same number of people who currently inhabit the planet.

For a long list of reasons, parents, teachers, and guidance counselors have begun to emphasize one specific form of education. At the expense of all the others.

In this country, it's widely believed that a 4 year degree for the most people.

Unfortunately, that's insane.

Of the 3 million available jobs today, less than *20%* require a 4 year degree.

The rest require training, and a willingness to learn a skill that's actually in-demand. On top of everything else, we have student loans outstanding in excess of $1 Trillion dollars.

In short, we're lending money we don't have to kids who can't pay it back so they can educate themselves for jobs that no longer exist.

That should probably stop.

iLikebigPayloads
Dr. Tyson,

What advice would you share to an undergraduate of physics and mathematics who is very uncertain about a future career in science? Some nights feel defeating from the course work alone, but the thought of a future career based on my education can be overwhelmingly intimidating.

I have no intentions of giving up because I am certain of one thing: learning and applying science fills me with joy.

I may be partly guilty for your scientific angst. Most of my public science persona involves conveying the joy of scientific discovery, and especially the joy of curiosity, from childhood through adulthood. What's commonly absent from my messaging is the steep investment of time and energy (physical and emotional) that becoming a scientist and actually doing science requires. In fact the struggle is what must be loved by aspiring scientists because being a practicing scientist requires this of you daily.

Not knowing the answer to a problem and struggling to find the answer is precisely what science is. It's neither more nor less than this. The fact that you are experiencing this very struggle is not a barrier to your progress it is the best evidence that you are on a path where you belong, if you love what you do.

Good luck. Sometimes you need that too.

LLFEELINGSASIDE
Life as we know it on earth is cell bases, DNA, and so on. If we did find alien life, are we sure we would recognize it? What if alien life is similar to iron, but our tests couldn't even detect some other unearthly element that makes it living. I guess my question is,

since earth life is so unique and specific to us, how do weexpect to recognize "life" so unique and specific to another world? Could we have seen life on a planet millions of light years away, but not realized it because the details of photography are limited?

Excellent question. We think life is alive and a slap of iron is not because, among a few other reasons, we have metabolism. We consume energy in the service of our existence. If we find any other entity that does this too, it would make a good candidate for life. Consider also that you reference and "unearthly" element. That is not likely at all because the periodic table of elements is full. There's no room for any other elements to be discovered in the natural universe. And using spectroscopy, we confirm that these very same elements are found in stars across the universe itself. Not only that, the four most common chemically active ingredients in the universe (H, He, O, C, N) are the SAME four most abundant ingredients in life on Earth. So our bias in searching for "life as we know it" is not entirely close-minded.

Jackanapes8
Hello Neil,

I work at a Christian school. One of my co workers (the science teacher) was banned from showing cosmos. The administrators who banned it (due to a parent complaint actually) refuse to watch it to judge for themselves.

What would you say to them to convince them to change their minds or reconsider?

In the USA, education is entirely local -- a surprise to most of the developed world. So a Christian school, or even a public school, could if they wanted to teach anything at all. It's just a matter of voting influence on a school board. If they fear the contents of Cosmos, they simply fear what science tells them about the natural world.

FYI: Galileo (a devout Christian) famously once said: "The Bible tells you how to go to heaven, not how the heaven's go.

So even he saw the line in the sand between the two. But this is 21st century America. And what matters here are the consequences of not teaching science to school children. Innovations in science and technology are the engines of tomorrow health, wealth, and security. So any school district that eschews the discoveries of science has disenfranchised itself from the future of civilization. They can still reap the benefits of it, but they will be paying to obtain (or gain access to) the discoveries of others, and no emergent industries will move their HQ there, if scientifically literate employees are nowhere to be found.

KillerTapeWorm

Hi Dr Tyson, huge fan. I know its a big question, but how do you go on knowing how small we are in this universe? The thought of my insignificance in the grand scheme of things tends to depress me as much as the vastness of the universe interests me. Thanks for your time!

Why should knowing we are indeed small in time, space, and size have anything to do with insignificance. Bacteria surely don't feel that way and they are billions of times smaller than us, yet they do most of our digesting. Ant's surely don't feel that way yet they likely represent nearly 20% of Earth's biomass. Why not instead think of how awesome it is that our 3lbs Human brain matter actually figured all this out. Why not look up to the clear night sky, and reflect on the fact that we don't simply live in this universe, but the universe lives within us -- through the atoms and molecules of our bodies, forged in the hearts of stars that long-ago gave their lives to the galaxy ... and to us. This is, of course, one aspect of the cosmic perspective that perhaps I and my astrophysics colleagues take for granted, but cannot be told often enough.

Codiene

I am not as intellectually inclined as I wish I was but I feel confident as a good orator and communicator having worked sales jobs.

I don't believe I have the capabilities to go into a STEM(science, technology, engineering and mathematics) degree so what do you think young people in my generation who cannot go into STEM should strive for?

also how'd you like the movie "Life"?

What matters in society is not how many STEM professionals are running around. What a boring world that would be if we were all scientists and engineers. The world needs poets and artists and actors and comedian, and politicians, and even lawyers. What i see is that if you like STEM, but for whatever reason will not become a STEM professional, you can still gain basic levels of science literacy in your life, and blend that awareness into your work. This is already happening in the Arts. There's no end of art installations, sitcoms, dramas, screenplays, first-run movies, that have been inspired by science. Including The Martian, which helped turn the word "Science" into a verb, and Avatar, the highest grossing film of all time. So if your will not become a scientist yourself, then do not hesitate to allow science to serve as the artist's muse. Next in line -- scientifically literate politicians.

North Korean Defector Sold Into Slavery in China (Experience) 15th October 2017

My name is Joy and I'm from North Korea. I escaped to China when I was 18 but was immediately trafficked and sold as a bride to a Chinese man for $3,000 USD. Life was difficult, but I gave birth to a daughter who became the joy of my life. After 2 years I was offered an opportunity to finally escape. I reached freedom through a 3,000-mile rescue route that brought me to Southeast Asia, and from there I flew to South Korea. Because the journey out of China is incredibly dangerous for North Koreans, I had to leave my daughter behind. I now live in South Korea and I am studying social work to help North Korean women who have also been trafficked. I hope to bring my daughter to South Korea to live with me one day.

Because I have family in North Korea that could face punishment if my identity was revealed, I cannot share my real name or show my face.

MrEuropaDiscoDancer
What is North Korea like? Is it anything like the news stories we see on the television? Is it better or worse? Are there any myths about North Korea that are spread by the western media? I'm guessing you didn't like it, hence the defection.
How likely is it you will see your daughter soon, and how will you be able to get her back?
What action can be taken to help stop human sex trafficking?

Good questions! There is so much focus in the western media about North Korea's military and nuclear weapons. There is rarely any stories about average North Koreans, especially those that live outside the capital Pyongyang. Most North Koreans are ordinary people that want to live peaceful lives but the media makes it look like every North Korean wants to destroy America or South Korea.

Everything in the underground broker networks revolves around money. North Korean women that cannot afford to cross the border are told it is free to cross and then when they cannot pay on the other side they are sold instead. That was my experience. If you want to get involved in helping North Korean women avoid sex trafficking you should fund rescues through organizations like LiNK. The safest way a woman can avoid being trafficked is to have her rescue paid for before she leaves the country. Then when she crosses she can enter a safe network that can move her out of China before she is exploited.

Keurum

What culture shocks did you face when you came to South Korea? And how different are the North and South Korean cultures? I'm thinking differences in body language, language, food, customs, values, beliefs, etc... How difficult/easy is it for a North Korean to adapt to Korean society? Is there a lot of discrimination towards North Koreas living in South Korea?

The first big cultural shock was when I saw South Korean women is very short skirts! North Korean culture is more socially conservative so I was very surprised to see couples in the South holding hands and kissing in public.

Korean society is very family oriented. It was very hard at first to adapt in the South when I didn't have a family to see or talk to anymore. On holidays I didn't know what to do because I had no family.

The South Korean language has so many strange words that are borrowed from English. That took some time to get used to!

It was also difficult to decide on what to study and what career to pursue. In North Korea, I didn't get to choose what my future would look like. It was kind of overwhelming to choose a path to take when there were so many choices.

Tagriel

How was your original escape to China orchestrated? Did your family help, and if not, how did you plan it as an 18-year-old with restricted contact with the outside world?

My step-mother wanted me to marry so I would not be her responsibility anymore. I heard rumors that I could escape to China and be adopted by an older Chinese couple and live a happy life there. My step-mother knew a broker who convinced me to go to China.

The broker guided me to the Tumen river and told me when and where to cross. When I was picked up on the other side the broker told me to pay for my escape or be sold as a bride. I had no money and was terrified of being arrested by the Chinese police. I felt so trapped.

LifeWin

All the news of North Korea is almost inconceivably dreadful. While I'm sure there is much misery in the country, can you tell us a story of a time when you or your family were genuinely happy? What sort of things bring joy to the average North Korean?

My fondest memories from North Korea revolve around my family. Everyday when my mom would come home she would give me a big hug and I loved that. I also have great memories of family talent shows where we would sign karaoke late into the night!

cicIope

1- What do you think about tourism companies offering trips to North Korea and the people that go on those trips? Do you think that it's just money that goes to the regime or that it helps in some way the locals?

2- Do you still have family in NK? If so, are you considering getting them out?

3- Have you met Yeonmi Park and Hyeonseo Lee? Do you relate to their stories?

4- Are you considering writing a memoir?

5- What city did you live in in NK? Did you ever have some kind of romantic relationship or held hands with someone?

I have kept a diary that I hope to one day turn into a book!

I do have family in North Korea and I get to talk to them often through special brokers that sneak Chinese phones into North Korea. If they wanted to come out I would help them but my grandmother is very old and my father is very sick and too weak to make the dangerous journey.

I do not want to disclose the city I lived in to protect my family but it was in the Northern part of the country.

aFamiliarStranger
My question is in regards to the suitcase that was in OJ's custody on the day he arrived from Chicago; later, Rob Kardashian walked away with it. I'm not asking for speculation on what was in it, but rather curious how big of a focal point it was for the prosecution team to obtain it? Do you think the state could have gotten the contents of the suitcase? And finally, how do you personally feel about about potential evidence walking out the front door for the "Trial of the Century"?M

Every time I see video of Simpson handing the Louis Vuitton bag to Kardashian, it makes me sick. We never learned the contents of the bag. I brought Kardashian to the Grand Jury and asked him about the bag under oath. There's nothing more I could say about that.

Notepadow
Loved your quote (paraphrasing) "OJ may have been a model prisoner but he's far from a model citizen." Priceless !
Moving forward, what advice would you give to other prosecutors trying similar high profile cases against celebrities? How can we preserve objectivity without making a mockery of the legal system?

I think that it's important to have available to those prosecutors a mental health professional and someone to manage the media and social media. I think that will help a prosecutor stay grounded and focused. If it's going to be a long trial – 8 moths, a year — I think it's important to have a nutritionist available. By the time the Simpson case was over, I'd lost more than 20 pounds and 2 teeth, had 4 root canals, and God knows what else.

Jh0102

What actor would you have liked to portray you on the television?

I don't know. I think that Sterling K. Brown is now me for the ages. I wrote the best book for that trial. My book was on the New York Times best seller list at #1 for weeks. However, no one in Hollywood discovered just how good it is. I think that 20 years ago, Denzel Washington would have made a good Chris Darden. I think that Tyrese Gibson would make a good Chris Darden if the series focused more on my personal life than my legal life. But I do hope one day somebody does do a movie about me and my life, perhaps just to enrich my children, if nothing else. But so far, people just steal my words and my images and don't even fucking bother to buy me a two-piece chicken snack at Popeyes.

Therealquiz
What is the greatest public misunderstanding about the work of a prosecutor?

I think it has more to do with prosecutors in general. I think it is a mistake to assume that because someone is a prosecutor, that he or she is somehow more honest or has more integrity just because they are a prosecutor. Most of the prosecutors I know are good people who are committed to protecting us from those who would prey on us. But these days, I sometimes run into prosecutors who just don't seem to have the character we used to have 20-30 years ago. People need to understand that prosecutors are lawyers, and like my grandmama once told me, a law degree is a license to lie.

3ach3r24
Do you feel OJ really put forth his best effort when trying on the glove? To me, it has always appeared that he bent his hand just enough to prevent the glove from sliding on.

Thank you. And no, he played around with it and tried to avoid making it fit. I hoped the jury would recognize that, but they couldn't see it, because they didn't want to see it.

IceCubeTrey55
What was the reaction of your family and friends after they learned you had taken the case?

I didn't really have any friends outside the DA's office. And a lot of those friends were supportive while others, even though they were prosecutors, went about the business of stabbing me in the back every chance they got. But that is the nature of lawyers — to consume their own.

VirtusAlpha48
Knowing what you know now and looking back on the case, would you have done anything different?

I would have done lots of things differently. First thing I would have done differently was to not announce beforehand that I intended to arrest O.J. By signaling to him that he was going to be arrested, it allowed him to get into his Bronco and take us on that slow speed Bronco chase.

FlashbackX
Is Fred Goldman's mustache as intimidating in real life as it is on TV?

Fred's mustache is created by God as the eighth wonder of the world, and there's something about Fred, that when he talks, you want to listen. He is a straight-shooter. He never minces words. And he is as good a man as his mustache looks on television.

Ino_things
Is it true that OJ could come out publicly now and say "yes, I did it. I killed them both" and nothing could be done about it?

Yes, that is true. He has been found innocent, and to prosecute him again in state court would constitute double jeopardy and would be precluded by law. Did I say innocent? I meant not guilty.

Pogiface

If you were walking down the street and saw OJ or he approached you, how would you feel? What would you say?

I wouldn't feel anything one way or the other. I sure as hell wouldn't be afraid of him. I'd probably tell him to get the fuck off my sidewalk and take his ass across the street.

Patrick Stewart (Actor/Entertainer)
20th August 2015

Shotbyelisa

- **What is your drink of choice?**
- **What is one of your favorite books you have read in the past year?**
- **What is the best worst thing that has happened to you? (i.e. a blessing in disguise)**
- **When is your next BFF date around NYC with Ian McKellen?**

- Favorite drink of choice is Oregon Pinot Noir.
- The letters of Vincent Van Gogh to his brother, Theo. Problem is, there are seven volumes and I've already been reading for two years.
- Best thing was meeting my wife, Sunny, and my soccer club, Huddersfield Town, failing to win a match so far this season was the worst.
- Nothing scheduled for NYC with my BFF. London, maybe.

Tattooedjenny
My question is whether you have done/would consider narrating audiobooks? I'm an audiobook junkie, and absolutely adore your voice.

I have done, but many decades ago. I'm afraid it is too labour intensive for the present state of my career. Maybe once I'm in retirement...perish the thought.

ConquerorWM
How did it feel to carry the Olympic Torch?

Unbelievably exciting. Unbelievable because I never expected it would happen to me and as an ex-athlete and huge fan of the Olympic Games, it was one of the best days of my life.

And, I ended the day taking home the torch, but I seem to have mislaid it. If anybody knows where it is, please let the @SirPatStew team know.

Bekausisaidso
What are some things on your bucket list?

My father retired from the military as Regimental Sergeant Major of the British Parachute Regiment. He jumped into action three times. I don't care for the action part of it, but I would love to experience what he did of jumping and parachuting safely to the ground.

The_tailor
What's your secret to staying so young, looking so good, and having so much fun? TELL US PLEASE!

Well the great man Sigmund Freud said the most important things for a happy and long life were love and work and I've had a cornucopia of both.

Georgiimichael
What's your favorite cocktail, sir?

A martini with Old Raj gin and very important, one olive. Who knew that you must never put an even number of olives in a martini glass. My son told me that martini drinkers are superstitious about even numbers of olives.

Shivan21
What would you advise to Daniel Radcliffe who'd like to play Shakespeare in theatre?

Then Daniel should do it wherever and whenever he can. But I warn him, he could get hooked and wave goodbye to a lovely film career.

IwalkedTheDinosaur
What has been your favorite role to voice act?

Deputy Director Avery Bullock on American Dad is my favorite role to voice act.

DandyBanana
Is there any project other than acting you've ever wanted to venture in to?

Yes! Deep-sea diving and mountaineering. There's something about going up and down that turns me on.

DarthSunshine
What's in your perfect sandwich?

Always, all my life, a favorite, thickly sliced Granny Smith apple on thick, heavily buttered white bread. Very healthy and yummy.

HoneyBadgerEXTREME
What was it like seeing your decapitated head in Macbeth?

Don't be silly, I couldn't see my head. It was decapitated!

Falcopatomus
If you HAD to have hair, what kind of hairstyle would you go with?

A mullet.

Fyodorkafka
Sir Patrick Stewart, I must say it's an honor to get the chance to speak with you. I was raised on The Next Generation, and I'd like to think the show imparted upon me a grand sense of imagination and wisdom. It's often stated that "The Inner Light" or the "Caymen" episode, is one of your favorites. I was hoping you could briefly describe your feelings about that episode and what about it resonated with you? For the rest of my life, I'll distinctly remember the scene where you hug the recorder after Riker leaves the room. Thank

you for inspiring me, for teaching me so much through Jean-luc.

Well, the thing is, my favorite episode is "Inner Light." It was a beautiful script, which for me was almost entirely located away from the Enterprise - and it's crew! And because I was given the chance to perform what Picard would have been like if his life experience had been different. But another important reason is that I had a son in that episode who was played by my son, Daniel Stewart. And if you care to see how he has grown up, watch my new series Blunt Talk.

Prisoner in a North Korean POW Camp For 10 Years (Experience) 30th March 2016

Javi404
What goes on day to day in the jail/concentration camps?

Has anyone gotten in-trouble from getting caught with USB sticks?

What other items are dropped such as books I would presume?

Daily life in the work camps is very mundane. We wake up at 5 am and are forced to work until sunset. We are given lessons on Kim il-sung and Juche. We are forced to watch public executions. We are physically abused - hit and tortured. I think of it as another form of Auschwitz. These work camps are like products of Nazism, and an abusive government needs elements such as Nazi concentration camps. They just have different ways of killing people.

People have almost gotten caught with the USB sticks. Thankfully, they managed to get out before they were caught. However, they cannot go back to North Korea now. But that's about it currently. North Korean citizens often get caught using these USB sticks but they are released when they give bribes to the police. I believe it would be about 500 dollars maximum in Pyeongang and about 200~300 dollars in other regions. The problem would be if they are caught and they have no money to bribe their way out.

DeusExChimera
Do you miss North Korea despite what you endured? And, is there any misconception about North Korea that you would like to share?

I dislike the North Korean government, not the people- so yes, I do miss the people there. North Koreans may seem different because they are brainwashed by the government;

but once their thoughts change through the flow of information, they are the same as anywhere else. I think it is lamentable that people think of the North Korean government and North Koreans as one entity. North Koreans may seem loyal to the government, but because they fear the government, they cannot speak their minds. For example, Seungjin Park, the North Korean soccer player during the World Cup, was at the Yoduk Political Prisoners Camp with me, but is now acting as the soccer team coach. However, he must hide the fact that he was at the prisoners camp. To learn more about North Korea, you must know something about the nature of North Korea. This is true even when visiting North Korea.

Markcubansotherwife
What kept you going?

When I was escaping, it was the early stages and there were no set escape routes. It was hard to defect without the help of the South Korean government. I had heard that you could live in places such as Harbin, China. However, I was hopeful that other paths would open. Missionaries came and prayed for us. The heavens helped me and I was able to board a ship that took me from China to South Korea.

AlabamaJesus
What is the ultimate end game here? How does the west need to respond to free the North Korean people?

The outside world seems to talk about putting 'pressure' on the North Korean government, but I don't think they know exactly what kind of pressure is necessary. Economic pressure is not the only type of pressure. People need to learn what the North Korean government fears the most. What they are doing to keep the government afloat. First, the government wants to prevent defection. They fear that if many people start to defect, a unification similar to the German case will take place. So, they are focused on keeping the border shut. Second, the government wants to prevent North Koreans from having access to outside information. The more North Korean citizens know, the more danger it is for the government. So far, I do not believe we have been targeting either of these. Real pressure on the North Korean government would be to open up the physical border and induce mass defection, or to open up the information barrier and to provide access to outside information. There needs to be a separation of the North Korean citizens from the government - for example, if more North Korean workers work abroad, they are not getting paid by the government and this eliminates their ties to the government.

Atouchofconsumption
Can you talk more about your efforts to disseminate free media inside North Korea? Does your organization use balloons sent over the DMZ? How far into the country do they travel? Is there ever push-back from the South Korean government because they are afraid your actions will further inflame tensions?

We don't use balloons. But I do think they play an important role. The South Korean, of course, tries to stop this method of spreading information because of possible political implications. The main thing about using flyers is to have a press conference about the information on the flyers. These flyers must be spread in secret. But the press conference must be held officially with many people and also have interviews. This is more stimulating for North Korea. Only the people near the DMZ have access to these flyers, unless the wind takes them further inland. We use movies, videos send the market to spread information. This way, information can be spread all over North Korea. I believe this to be a the greatest method of changing the way North Koreans think. Spreading information through media is very important.

MayerR
What is your view on westerners visiting North Korea as part of a tour and giving money back to the regime?

I think that the government does benefit a little bit from the money gained through the tours Westerners take to North Korea. I don't think that it is a bad idea to experience and see North Korea this way. However, currently, foreign visitors are getting arrested by the government and are used as pieces for negotiation, so refraining from visiting North Korea seems wise. I think that the North Korean government are using these tourists as a method of negotiation with foreign governments (ie. the Canadian pastor and the American student). Because the government is receiving internal and external pressure, they are using these tourists as hostages for negotiation, because they are unstable. So currently, I think it is better to refrain from visiting North Korea.

RL Stein (Author)
31st October 2016

Squidjib
Did you ever have any input on the covers of the original 62 books? Tim Jacobus' art remains iconic. They really need to put out a coffee table book of those covers!

Tim's covers were amazing. I always sent him short summaries of the stories. He painted at the same time I was writing the book.

Angeluscado

1. **Who is your favourite horror author, besides yourself?**
2. **How do you feel about the Goosebumps TV show that aired in the '90's?**

I'm a big Stephen King fan. I think he's a terrific storyteller. I also like Peter Straub

Hawkofglory
How often do you look back at a book, and wish you had done something differently?

I always wish I had done something differently, but I seldom look back at books. Gotta move on to the next one. By the way, the new Fear Street book is called The Dead Boyfriend. I'm enjoying writing Fear Street again. And watch for a Fear Street movie next year!

Mikerapin
Have you ever considered writing for comic books?

I'm writing a series of comic books for Marvel-- my first comics ever. But I'm not allowed to talk about them yet.

Suaveitguy
How do you begin writing a story? How much is Romantic inspiration and how much is pragmatic design/planning?

All of my stories start with a title. The title leads me to the story.

Isiahcomedian
Who did you read growing up?

I read mostly comics--Tales from the Crypt, The Vault of Horror, MAD. When I was nine, I discovered Ray Bradbury. Changed my life.

Nifkinten
Which book of yours is your favorite?

My favorite GB book is he Haunted Mask. I also enjoy writing the Slappy books-- he's so evil, he's fun to write.

Juggilinjnuggala
What was the worst character you've ever written?

Jellyjam from Camp Jellyjam. He smelled so bad, he died of his own odor.

Mrzonules
Hey Mr. Stine!! What's your favorite Halloween candy?
I'm very loyal to the KitKat Bar.

Suaveitguy
What do you think of Rod Serling's work?

Rod Serling was a hero of mine. The Twilight Zone was a big influence on me. I've seen them all.

Din7
What literary works influence you the most?

Stephen King, Agatha Christie, Ray Bradbury, Harlan Coben, P.G. Wodehouse....

rronBlack
What do you think the scariest movie of all time is?

The Shining.

MattBaster
***Ermahgerd**, thank you for doing this AMA! I've read that instead of getting scared, you laugh at horror movies. With that in mind, what is the "funniest" movie you've ever seen?*

The Rink with Charlie Chaplin Duck Soup with the Marx Brothers The Naked Gun.

Asappringles
Do you like mustard?

Why are you asking this? Do you have a thing about mustard?

Robert Downey Jr (Actor)
7th October 2014

Logicatch
Your portrayal as Kirk Lazarus in Tropic Thunder was, in my opinion, one of the best comedic performances of all time, but it must have felt like a very risky role to take on. Did you have any fears about how the character would be perceived? What did you do to prepare yourself for the role?

Fortunately, it's about an affably self-important white guy who thinks he understands the "black experience." It was *so* wrong and outrageous that it was forgivable. But I certainly was happy to hear from my African-American friends that they were okay with it, and some of them even delighted in telling me what relative it reminded them of. Somebody just told me just the other day that they're convinced that I was channeling Wesley Snipes. He's a pretty cool customer, so I don't want to presume I would be up to the task.

Rdjfan
In the last few years, it seems like the media has increasingly identified you with the character of Tony Stark. Can you talk about what that's like, and how you hold onto your identity in the face it it?

Let me try.
The first Iron Man was essentially wrapping the character around a cooler version of "me." As we've gone along, I'm starting to wonder who's playing who, and I'm glad there are so many talented new people in the Marvel lineup. Ultimately, I'm real, and he's not. It's kind of important for me to remember that.

PianoWhore
Being such a big star I imagine that you get many people asking for autographs etc. I was wondering

what is the strangest or most memorable fan encounter that you've had?

I *love* running into kids who didn't expect to see me. I once ran into a four year old who just happened to be wearing a Captain America mask at the time. It seemed natural to him, being that he was Cap, to see some of his friends around. I think I was more excited than him.

For the most part, autograph collectors are pretty cool, and when they're weird, you just try to forget them.

Jebuz60
Thank you for making kiss kiss bang bang. Very underrated. What's your favorite story about making that film?

It was entirely shot at night. We were pretty giddy most of the time. I saw it last week by chance, and had a flood of fond memories. On the first day of shooting, Val Kilmer (genius) almost choked to death on a piece of catering chicken *right* before we shot the first scene of the movie. His eyes were still watering until we got to his close up.

I'm so happy he's still with us.

Eddog21
I am a big fan of yours, and really loved your roles in Iron Man And the Avengers, as well as Tropic thunder, of course. Other than asking for an autograph, which I'd totally love, I wanted to ask you how you deal with stress, and what are good ways to prevent stressful situations?

It's important to remember to eat, catch yourself when you're getting irritable, recognize when you're feeling lonely, and not burn out when you're tired.

Zedab
You've spoken before about your willingness to re-don the Iron Man Armor if Mel Gibson was to direct. First of all, on a scale of 1 to 11 how serious were you? Secondly, what do you think Mel Gibson would bring to

**the Iron Man series and would you still consider
returning if he does not direct?**

It was an offhanded remark to a journalist and friend. I have
other projects in mind for Mel and I - sooner than later the
Marvel Roster will be made public and *all* questions will be
answered.

Bleek213
**Just watched back to school the other day; were you
cool with wearing all of the extreme clothing? And what
was it like to work with Rodney Dangerfield?**

Rodney Dangerfield was a *true* original. *Extremely* kind.
Wickedly funny. *Forget* the costumes - I had more gelatine in
my hair than you'd use for 100 bowls of Jell-O! You could
literally bounce a tennis ball off my hair. It was crispy - it
turned into, like, they were like bamboo horns. It was the
best.

Darabfox
How is it that your facial hair is always on point?

chuckle
Excellent question.

It started with the first Iron Man: a guy named Pedro from
Shave of Beverly Hills. I mean, this guy's an artist. He's like
the Edward Scissorhands of Mustaches and Beards. And *then*,
once you set a standard, it's all about upkeep and modulating
it. It tends to be a lot of work, but I'm glad you appreciate it.

Cwatts7283
What is your favorite memory from filming Bowfinger?

I remember driving a classic convertible, first day of shooting,
no experience with the car, it was a big boat, and I have to fit
it right into a parking spot with a sandbag, that sort of thing.
And I remember being so proud that i didn't bang up the car,
or overshoot the mark and knock over the monitors or
something.

Globochememployee
If you could develop any book into a movie, what would it be and why? Which character would you play?

Gore Vidal wrote an excellent novel around 1962, about an emperor, Julian. I believe he was just after Constantine and Constantius, so roughly 4th Century Common Era (A.D.). I'm too old to play him, but it's an incredible story.

break-kay
Do you feel like playing two major sarcastic/disrespectful/buck authority characters in Sherlock and Tony Stark has colored the roles you are offered/take? I see your character in the Judge is the same vein as well. Or are you just playing yourself in all these movies and you just change clothes?

chuckle

The Judge is a departure of sorts in that Hank starts off in a way audiences might compare to other roles, but there's a significant change and an eventual humility.

I think Tony and Sherlock are pretty dissimilar, and always strive to not seem like a guy who's fascinated with playing himself, regardless of the character.

Ronda Rousey (Sports)
10th August 2015

Knuckledork

What is your sincere opinion about Cyborg?

How do you think your fight against Tate and hopefully Cyborg will play out assuming perfect physical and mental condition from both sides?

Do you think you would legitimately beat Floyd Mayweather in a ruleless fight?

What do you have to say about Mike Tyson's rumored return to the ring?

How do you think Fedor Emelianenko will do in the octagon after all these years of absence?

Thanks for the AMA, much love and the best of luck to you in the future.

Sincere opinion about Cyborg: she's just waiting to be offered enough money to get her ass kicked ('cuz she *knows* she'll get her ass kicked). I know for a fact she can make the weight. She consulted with Mike Dolce (my current nutritionist) before I ever started working with him and after consulting with her he said he could get her in "the best shape of her life" at 135. She then started being represented by Tito Ortiz and all talk stopped. The delay is all about money, not her weight. She made 145 pumped full of steroids. She can healthily make 135 without them. Her shows that she headlines lose thousands of dollars, and the majority of the tickets are given away because no one will buy them. She *needs* me. So pretty much we're waiting for her to realize that she needs to fight me before I retire or she'll never have enough money to retire. I would like me kicking her ass be my retirement fight but whether she steps up or not I'll walk away undefeated and happily ever after regardless.

Do I think I would legit beat Mayweather in a ruleless fight? Floyd is one of the best boxers of all time. He would definitely beat me in a boxing match. I unfortunately don't get into "matches". I *fight* for a living. In a no rules fight, I believe I can beat anyone on this planet. Boxing is a sweet science with strict rules that I respect very much and aspire every day to improve at. But you said ruleless fight, and that's my honest answer.

I'd be surprised if Mike Tyson returned to the ring but could imagine he would do it in a charity kind of capacity, and if so good for him.

Ring rust is a real serious thing that is hard to overcome and of course I wish Fedor the best but that much of a lay off would affect anyone's performance, which is why I fight so often.

Runstacey
I'm incredibly inspired by your eating disorder recovery through UFC. When I was struggling with anorexia, I felt so weak and powerless, and feel so strong after recovery. How does it feel to conquer something so daunting? I feel like it makes you invincible!

Thanks for the kind words. It feels very liberating to free of the guilt that used to come with every meal. And I feel like I have so much extra space in my brain now that I'm not constantly thinking about the next meal and trying to eat as much as possible every day while still losing weight. I feel amazing. I (think) I look amazing. And I just ate some bomb-ass french toast this morning. I'm so happy to hear about all the progress you've made on yourself and best of luck for the future.

Saraeveg
Hi Ronda! I recently discovered that you had Childhood Apraxia of Speech (CAS) growing up. I'm a new speech therapist and a huge fan. Do you feel as though overcoming CAS helped you become the tenacious fighter we know you are today? Is there any message you'd like to send to kids out there struggling with speech? I'd also love to know what you liked/didn't about speech therapy, and what you wished your speech therapist said or did for you.

I love my speech therapist – I thought she was super cool and I didn't even know I was in speech therapy. I'd like to tell any kid struggling with speech that anything can be overcome with hard work regardless of how insurmountable the odds seem. Shout out to all speech therapists. You're all awesome. And the best thing about my recovery was that I was never allowed to feel interior.

Larock
Hi Ronda,

With your exponential increase recently in exposure and recognition, do you worry about the amount of control that the media has over your image? And have you run into circumstances where you felt you were misrepresented or portrayed inaccurately by the media?

I accept that I have NO control over my image already. So, I try not to let the state of my perception have any effect on my happiness. You can never truly know anyone through only media anyway. If anything I just try to keep in mind that I'm an entertainer and not a politician or Miss America.

Iceomatic69
Favourite male fighter to watch in the UFC?

Demetrious Johnson. I think he's the most well-rounded and I feel like I'm watching one of the later episodes of Dragon Ball Z when you only see one second of action going on between them disappearing 'cuz they're going so damn fast. I wouldn't be surprised if rocks start levitating around the ring because of all the energy emanating from it. Mighty Mouse vs. Dominick Cruz was one of my favorite (and most under-appreciated) fights ever.

Simon Pegg and Nick Frost (Writer/Actor)
20th August 2013

Drocks27

Simon and Nick:

1) When did you know it was love?

2) How has life changed now that you are both married and "settled down"

Simon, Nick and Edgar

3) What was the funniest moment you have had filming a movie together?

4) How did you come up with the idea of "conformity" being a part of all of your movies?

1) Almost immediately I think when we met. When we met we became good friends very quickly and I think it was immediately apparent to us that there was chemistry.

2) Lot better.

3) We work very hard, we don't do it to mess around and we enjoy what we do, but we have to focus. Too much messing about on set can be detrimental to the process. So yes, it's huge fun but to have to pick a single moment, we loved it all.

4) With the film it's about an idea of something being forced on someone - maybe it's part of being British, or on the fringes of the filmmaking process, but it's something that appeals to us as a storytelling device.

Tfu09

At the end of Shaun of the Dead, do you think Shaun ever got around to taking Liz out to Fulci's?

Absolutely. Yes he did, and they had a lovely meal. Shaun had some linguine and some chianti. She had a starter but not more than that since she was trying to lose weight.

Alxf

Where did the "Come On, Eileen" scene with Brian in Spaced come from? Based on a true experience? It introduced me to the song, and my life is infinitely better for it.

No it was based on the idea that back in the '80s the bars and clubs were more dangerous than before Ecstasy appeared. After which, there was a cessation in violence in nightclubs. Not saying that's a good thing but that's what it was.

Rokuthirteen
The World's End has quite a bit of beer in it. What are your favourites?

Are you football/soccer fans? And if so, who do you support?

I don't drink so that's my answer.
I would rather drink bleach than watch soccer.

Yo_mumma
What are your weapons of choice in a zombie apocalypse?

You have to go with blunt objects. Guns are very well but you have to reload them, and they are going to run out of ammo, so blunt objects - always always always [Simon]

I would have to say a sword. A long broadsword. So you're far enough away that they can't bite you. Failing that, genetics. Maybe we could just find a way to cure them.[Nick]

ImNoSuperman45
What is each of your favourite bands?.

I like The London Boys. I don't listen to anything else.[Simon]
Erasure... and The Eurythmics.[Nick]

Steve Wozniak (Technology)
16th March 2016

NiwhsregegroeG
What is your favorite up and coming gadget? Anything people don't know about yet?

Well, I would think probably one of them is certainly the Oculus Rift, or any of the VR headsets. I love putting mine on and watching a basketball game live; it was just an experience that you can't believe. Sometimes I come out of a VR world, take off the helmet, and I can't believe I'm actually sitting in my office, at a desk at home. So, that's one of the big ones.

Right now, Amazon Echo; it's getting so popular among the people that use it and they speak so highly of it, and it's so inexpensive. I see a lot of developers that went into smartphones jumping onto that. It's a platform, and when you have a platform that everybody else is writing apps for and connecting to, basically they're advertising your company as much as you are.

Obviously, I'm very interested in the evolution of self-driving cars. Right now, the assist that they give you for keeping in your lane and cruise control...the cruise control started back in 2004 actually, adjusting your distance. I love driving my Tesla so much, I just smile! I sit there in the driver's seat, and I kinda look over at my wife, and I just smile. I'm so happy, not using my hands or feet. So, I think the progression towards self-driving cars is going to be a good one. But it falls into that category of AI.

Now, the AI that impresses me, I fell in love 10 years ago - well not 10 years ago, but whenever it started; Siri was an app you could buy for the iPhone, and I bought it. And for one year, Apple didn't have it. I just spoke of it as the app that changed my life, because I get to live as a human, saying things out of my head the way I would to another human, and a machine understands me. And I have wanted that to be the future for...forever.

Actually, ever since our Newton message pad, where I could type in, "Sara, dentist, Tuesday, 2 PM," and click the assist button, and it would open up the calendar; Tuesday at 2 PM, it would put the word *dentist*, and it would grab *Sara* out of my contact list. I hand wrote with my own muscles a message for myself, for a human, and a machine understood me. So, I want that to get better and better; machines understanding what we mean, so that we can eventually communicate with them as our best, most trusted friends that know our own hearts and souls better than other humans.

Sobernoob3
What do you consider the most difficult obstacle you've ever had to overcome?

I had an easy life. I was so good in math, science, electronics, computers, way ahead of the world, that I would never have to worry about a job. So, I didn't even have obstacles of, *how am I going to get a good job or do these things?*

Certainly in my early design days, I sometimes tackled problems that I didn't know if it was possible to solve, but when I'd get there I'd try to look for a solution, and somehow I always found it. Magic was pouring out of me, back in those days.

In later times, well, I've had divorces. So I guess you could say those are obstacles in life that I regret. But sometimes you grow up with a geekish personality that isn't really very social, and I dunno, you wind up in places you shouldn't have been.

Let's see, other obstacles...I described one earlier about a product I was trying to make, to locate things like pets and cars and briefcases. The obstacles that I ran into were whether I could come up with some magic ideas. And I did come up with at least one magic idea, but it didn't achieve the results I wanted in terms of price, power usage, and size.

Basically I think obstacles do a lot with dealing with people, and I work very independently, as far as I can, and then turn it over to others in very complete forms. So I didn't have a lot of the obstacles some people would talk about.

Obviously in business, we ran into obstacles at Apple. We all believed so much in doing the right thing, and building the Macintosh for the future rather than keeping with the dumb old computers of the past, and trying to achieve the world market. You know, holding our percentage of the world market as it grew ten times. We let Microsoft have all that growth, because we believed in doing the right things. Would you ever look back and say you regretted it or it was an obstacle? No. It was something we had to work hard to finally build a Macintosh market, and get our company back. But, we did the right thing.

Tiger_Style36

What is your opinion on how immersive our technology is becoming? We use computers in some form, almost constantly. Do you ever feel in your own life you that it becomes overwhelming?

I have that feeling all the time because I like a nice, quiet, simple life. I grew up shy. I'm more into products than I'm into socializing. And I do not carry around my phone answering every text message instantly. I am not one of those people.

I wait until I'm alone in my places and get on my computer and do things where I think I'm more efficient. I really see a lot of people that are dragged into it, but you know, I don't criticize them. When you have change, it's not that the change in how people are behaving different to you is bad or good, it's just different.

So that's sort of the modern way, and you know the millennials, every generation wants to criticize the next generation for missing out on things like personal human contact, but I'll tell you a little story. When we started Apple, Steve Jobs and I talked about how we wanted to make blind people as equal and capable as sighted people, and you'd have to say we succeeded when you look at all the people walking down the sidewalk looking down at something in their hands and totally oblivious to everything around them!

Clydethechicken

Hi! First off, you are my greatest idol :) I was wondering, why did you leave Apple?

Hi Clyde, thanks. I left Apple partly because i wanted to be, like, a normal person. I didn't want to seek wealth and power, because in my mind it often corrupts people, and I didn't want to be that person who runs a company. The first time I left Apple was an odd accident. I had a plane crash as a pilot. I didn't come out of an amnesia state for five weeks where I didn't know time was passing. When I came out of the amnesia I realized that the Macintosh team (they were my favorite, most creative thinking team at Apple, and I was on that team), would be fine without me.

So I called up Steve Jobs and told him "Macintosh team's in great shape, I'm gonna go back to college and get my degree." I had one year left to go. If I waited another year it would be too late to ever go back to college again actually. So I went back to Berkeley under the fake name Rocky Raccoon Clark, and that's what it says on my Berkeley diploma. That was the first time I left Apple. I came back and worked as an engineer. When the Macintosh project failed we had to recover with some Apple II projects, took us into the Apple IIGS to keep some money coming into the company for a while as we built the Macintosh market. And then I left the second time because I love startups. I love just a group of two or three or five people talking about an idea and going out and making it a reality. It may not be all the millions and billions of dollars in the world, but it's something you're doing yourself. The idea I came up with was for the first universal remote control, the CL 9 Core, so I left Apple to build that.

www.ingramcontent.com/pod-product-compliance
Lightning Source LLC
Chambersburg PA
CBHW051319220526
45468CB00004B/1406